Dwayne's Guitar Lessons Presents:

Demystifying the Blues Scales

By

Dwayne Jenkins

Introduction

Welcome to "Demystifying The Blues Scales"! A player's guide designed to help guitarists of all levels unlock the mystery of blues scales and enhance their playing. Through a structured approach, you'll explore the depths of blues music.

Learning concepts and techniques used by key players of the genre to elevate your guitar skills to the next level. Carefully helping you to unravel the mysteries of the blues and gain mastery over the fretboard.

Whether you're a novice or a seasoned guitarist seeking to refine your technique, this guide is designed to provide you with the essential tools and insights needed to master the universal language of emotion.

Blues music is more than just a genre; it's a profound form of expression that has influenced countless musical styles and artists across the globe. Originating from the African-American communities in the Deep South.

The blues is a cultural expression of storytelling and is characterized by its distinct scales, chord progressions, and techniques that convey the depth and complexity of human emotion.

In this guide, you will embark on a journey through the rich landscape of blues music, exploring fundamental techniques that form the backbone of blues guitar, such as string bending, vibrato, and slides.

These techniques will infuse your playing with the soul and expressiveness that define the blues. Including the essential scales like the minor and major pentatonic scales, which serve as the foundation for crafting authentic blues solos.

Through step-by-step lessons that build upon themselves for better comprehension, you will gain the ability to create compelling solos, incorporating improvisation and expressive techniques to convey emotion to connect with your audience.

So, grab your guitar, embrace the soulful essence of the blues, and let this guide lead you to new levels of creativity and expression. Welcome to the world of blues guitar mastery. Let's get started!

Dwayne Jenkins

Table of Contents

Chapter 1 Understanding the Basics

Lesson 1: The Origins of Blues Music

The blues is a music genre that originated in the African-American communities of the Deep South of the United States around the end of the 19th century. Its roots trace back to African musical traditions, work songs, and folk music.

The blues have been a powerful means of expression, often reflecting the struggles, hopes, and emotions of those who created and played it.

Influences on Modern Music

The influence of blues music extends far beyond its origins, having played a critical role in the development of rock and roll and other modern music genres. Understanding the history of the blues provides valuable insight into its impact.

Key Figures in Blues History

Some of the pivotal figures in blues history include legends such as Robert Johnson, B.B. King, Muddy Waters, and Howlin' Wolf. Their contributions not only defined the sound of blues music but also inspired countless musicians across various genres.

The Evolution of Blues Music

Over the decades, the blues has evolved, incorporating elements from other musical styles and adapting to cultural changes. From the early Delta blues to the electrified Chicago blues, it remains a dynamic and influential genre that continues to resonate with audiences worldwide.

Jimi Hendrix, Jimmy Page, and Stevie Ray Vaughan (SRV) each played pivotal roles in elevating the blues by blending traditional blues elements with innovative techniques and electrifying performances.

Hendrix revolutionized guitar playing through his use of feedback, distortion, and the wah-wah pedal, creating a sound that was groundbreaking and deeply rooted in blues.

The ability to fuse blues with psychedelic rock expanded the genre's reach and inspired countless musicians like Jimmy Page, with Led Zeppelin, who infused blues with hard rock, crafting timeless riffs and solos that introduced blues to a new generation of listeners.

His dynamic guitar work, characterized by powerful riffs and intricate solos, demonstrated the blues' adaptability and enduring appeal.

Meanwhile, Stevie Ray Vaughan revitalized the blues with his passionate playing and soulful expression, bridging the gap between traditional blues and contemporary rock.

His virtuosic guitar skills and emotional depth resonated with audiences, reaffirming the blues' relevance in modern music.

Together, these artists not only preserved the blues' legacy but also propelled it into new and exciting directions, ensuring its continued influence and popularity.

By exploring the rich history and origins of blues music, you will gain a deeper appreciation for its significance and the profound impact it has had on music as a whole.

Lesson 2: Essential Guitar Techniques

To truly master the blues, it's imperative to build a solid foundation of essential guitar techniques. This lesson will guide you through the fundamental techniques that every blues guitarist should know, setting the stage for more advanced playing as you progress.

1. String Bending

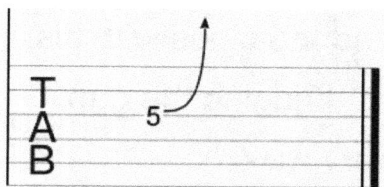

String bending is a quintessential technique in blues guitar, allowing you to add expressive, vocal-like qualities to your playing.

By bending the string, you can achieve notes that are not available through standard fretting, creating a soulful and emotive sound.

- **Basic Bend:** Start with a half-step bend, and progress to a full-step bend as you gain confidence.
- **Pre-Bend and Release:** Bend the string to the desired pitch before striking it, then release it back to the original pitch.

2. Vibrato

Vibrato adds richness and depth to your notes, giving them a singing quality. It involves subtly varying the pitch of a sustained note by moving the fretting hand back and forth.

- **Wrist Vibrato:** Use the wrist to create a smooth, controlled vibrato.
- **Finger Vibrato:** Similar to wrist vibrato but primarily uses finger movement for a more nuanced effect.

3. Slides

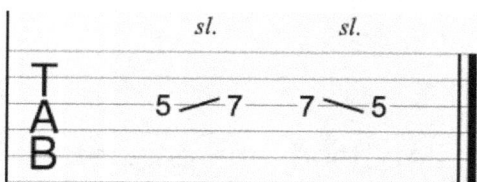

Slides are used to transition smoothly between notes, creating a fluid, seamless sound. They can be applied both to single notes and entire phrases.

- **Ascending Slide:** Start on a lower note and slide up to the target note.
- **Descending Slide:** Begin on a higher note and slide down to the desired note.

4. Hammer-Ons and Pull-Offs

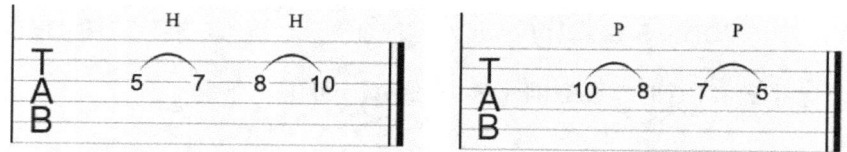

These techniques are used to play notes in quick succession without picking each one, adding speed and fluidity to your playing.

- **Hammer-On:** Strike a note and then "hammer" your finger onto a higher fret.
- **Pull-Off:** Play a note, then pull your finger off the string to let a lower note ring.

5. Trills

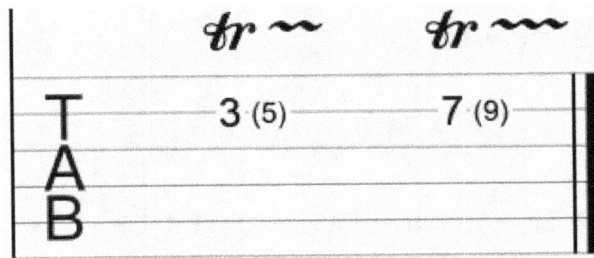

Trills are repeated hammer-ons and pull-offs without using your picking hand for both notes, which creates an effect that adds rhythm and texture to your playing.

- **Repeated Trills:** Use this technique with multiple notes and move up or down the fretboard.

By mastering these essential techniques, you'll have the tools you need to start expressing yourself through blues guitar. Practice each technique, focus on precision and control, before gradually increasing your speed.

Lesson 3: Introduction to Blues Scales

In this lesson, you'll be introduced to the fundamental blues scales that form the backbone of blues guitar playing. By understanding and mastering these scales, you'll provide yourself with the tools to create authentic blues sounds and express your musical ideas effectively.

1. The Basic Blues Scale

The basic blues scale is a variation of the major or minor pentatonic scale, with an added note known as the "blue note," which gives the scale its distinctive sound. This scale is essential for crafting the characteristic blues feel.

- **Structure:** The blues scale consists of six notes. In the key of A minor, for example, the notes are A, C, D, Eb, E, and G.
- **Blue Note:** The Eb (or D#) is the blue note, adding tension and emotion to your playing.
- Ascending the scale, a note is considered sharp, whereas descending the scale, a note is considered flat.

So Eb is the same as D#, just depending on which way you are moving along the scale. This can be a bit confusing if this is not known. C# is the same as Db, F# is the same as Gb, etc.

A Major: A B C# D E F# G# = 1 2 3 4 5 6 7

A Minor: A B C D E F G = 1 2 b3 4 5 b6 b7

A Minor Blues: A C D Eb E G = 1 b3 4 b5 5 b7

2. Major Blues Scale

While the minor blues scale is more widely used, the major blues scale also offers a unique sound that can bring a brighter, more upbeat feel to your music.

- **Structure:** Similar to the minor scale with a blue note added. But this time it is the flat 3rd note.
- **Applications:** Use the major blues scale to create a happier, more optimistic mood in your blues playing.

C Major Scale : C D E F G A B C = 1 2 3 4 5 6 7

C Major Blues: C D Eb E G A = 1 2 b3 3 5 6

See how the blues scale comes out of the major and minor.

3. Combining Scales

An effective blues guitarist often combines both the major and minor blues scales to create interesting and dynamic solos. This blending allows for greater expressiveness and variety in your music.

- **Transitioning:** Practice moving smoothly between the minor and major blues scales to enhance your solos.
- **Experimentation:** Try incorporating both scales into your improvisation to see how they can complement each other.

4. Practicing Blues Scales

To master these scales, dedicate time to practicing them in different keys and positions across the fretboard. This will enhance your flexibility and confidence in using them during performances or improvisation.

- **Scales in Different Keys:** Start with the key of C major. This is the easiest scale to work with.
- Then practice in other keys like E, G, and A major.

- **Fretboard Familiarity:** Then work on playing in A minor. Notice the difference between the two keys.
- Play the natural major, the natural minor, and both major and minor blues variations.
- Playing in various positions will give you a comprehensive understanding of the fretboard.

By the end of this lesson, you should have a solid foundation in the essential blues scales necessary for blues guitar playing. These scales will serve as the building blocks for creating expressive solos and developing your unique blues sound.

Lesson 4: Building Your Blues Vocabulary

To become a proficient blues guitarist, it's essential to develop a rich vocabulary of musical phrases and licks. This lesson will help you expand your repertoire by introducing you to key blues phrases that are foundational to the genre.

1. Understanding Blues Phrasing

Blues phrasing is the art of combining notes and rhythms to create expressive and compelling musical statements. A well-crafted blues phrase can convey deep emotion and connect with your audience on a personal level.

- **Call and Response:** This technique involves creating a musical conversation, where one phrase (the "call") is answered by another (the "response"). This is a hallmark of blues music and can add a dynamic element to your playing.
- **Use of Space:** Silence is as important as sound in blues phrasing. Learn to use pauses effectively to create tension and emphasize certain notes.

2. Common Blues Licks

Blues licks are short, memorable phrases that can be used as building blocks for solos and improvisation. Familiarize yourself with these essential licks to enhance your blues vocabulary.

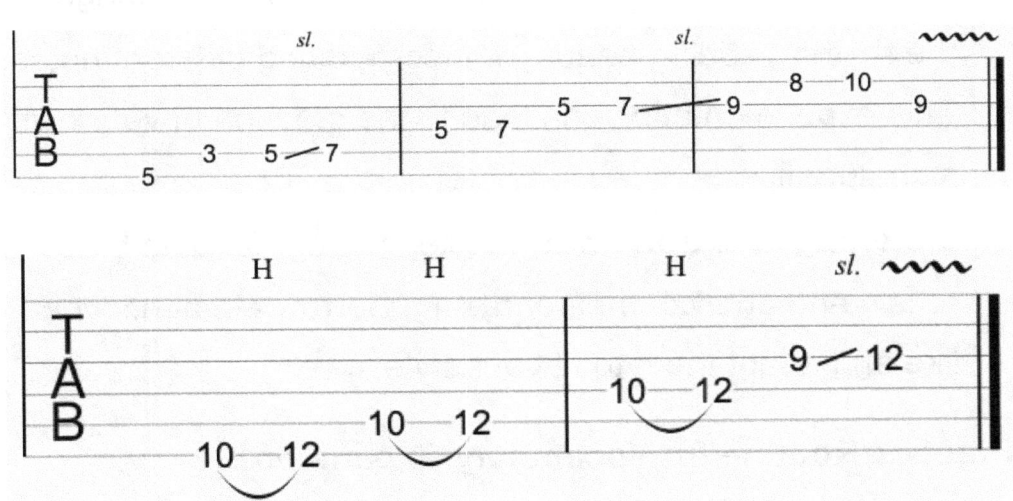

These are classic guitar lick examples using common techniques associated with lead guitar.

- **Classic Turnaround Lick:** Often used at the end of a 12-bar blues progression, this lick helps transition back to the beginning of the progression smoothly.
- **B.B. King Style Box Lick:** A simple yet powerful lick that uses note repetition and vibrato to create a soulful sound.

3. Developing Your Own Licks

While learning classic licks is important, developing your own unique phrases is essential for personal expression.

- **Experimentation:** Try altering existing licks by changing the rhythm, adding bends, or incorporating different notes. This experimentation can lead to the creation of your own signature licks.
- **Listening and Borrowing:** Listen to your favorite blues artists and analyze their phrasing. Borrow elements you like and adapt them to fit your style.

4. Practice Routine for Vocabulary Expansion

Consistent practice is key to expanding your blues vocabulary. Here's a suggested routine to incorporate into your practice sessions:

- **Daily Lick Practice:** Dedicate time each day to learning and perfecting a new lick. Focus on precision and feel.
- **Integrate Licks into Solos:** Practice using these licks within your solos to ensure they become a natural part of your playing.
- **Record and Review:** Record your practice sessions and listen back to identify areas for improvement and track your progress.

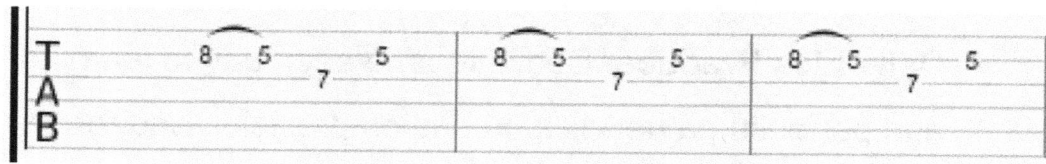

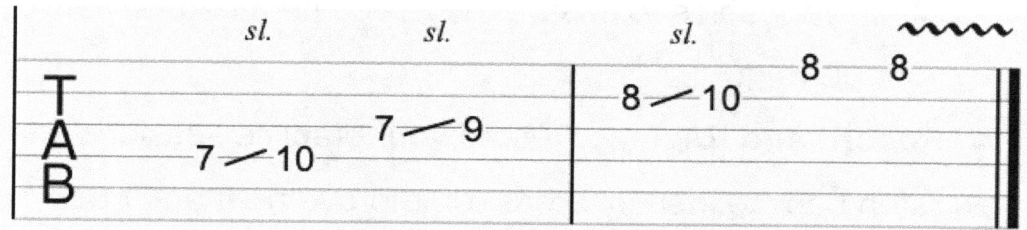

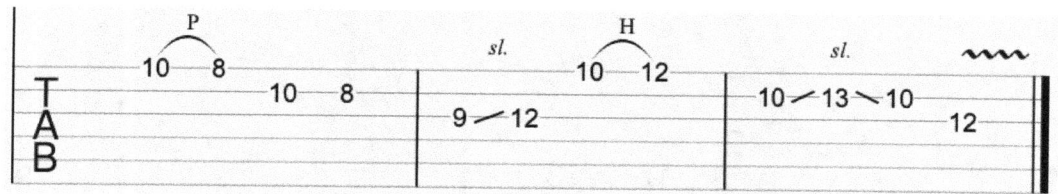

Go through these examples, and you'll get familiar wth using the techniques you learned earlier in phrasing examples.

By the end of this lesson, you should have a broadened blues vocabulary that you can draw upon to create expressive and memorable solos. This foundation will enable you to communicate your musical ideas more effectively and develop your own unique voice within the blues genre.

Lesson 5: Chapter 1 Quiz

Test your knowledge of Chapter 1 by answering the following questions. This will make sure you build a solid foundation and are ready for the next chapter.

Q: What are the origins of blues music and its influence?
A: _____

Q: Who are the three key figures who elevated the blues?
A: _____

Q: What are some techniques used in blues guitar playing?
A: _____

Q: How is the major blues different from the major?
A: _____

Q: How is the minor blues different from the natural minor?
A: _____

Q: What is phrasing, and why is it important in the blues?
A: _____

Q: What is the benefit of playing blues scales in multiple keys?
A: _____

Chapter 1 Summary

In this first chapter, we have covered some of the basics. This will set the foundation for all future studies. From this book and other books, you will learn in the future.

First, you learned about the origins of blues music. This is where it started, its influence on modern music, and key players that enhanced its exposure.

Second, you learned about essential guitar techniques that are commonly used for playing blues solos. String bending, slides, hammer-ons, pull-offs, and vibrato.

Third, you are introduced to the basics of blues scales. This is the addition of the "blue" note. This will be present in both the minor and major blues scales.

Fourth, you learned about building your blues vocabulary. This would be blues phrasing, call and response, and blues licks with examples.

Fifth, you went through a learning assessment to make sure you know the chapter well and build a solid foundation of these concepts.

Chapter 2 Mastering The Minor Pentatonic

Lesson 6: The Minor Pentatonic Scale

The minor pentatonic scale is a fundamental tool for guitarists, especially in blues music. Understanding its structure will provide you with a solid foundation for improvisation and soloing.

It is widely used in various music genres, particularly blues, rock, and jazz, due to its simplicity and versatility. Since we went through the A minor already, we will look at this again in G minor.

- **Structure:** The scale consists of the root note, minor third, perfect fourth, perfect fifth, and minor seventh.
- **Example in G Minor:** The notes in G minor pentatonic would be G, Bb, C, D, and F.

G Major: G A B C D E F# = 1 2 3 4 5 6 7

G Minor: G A Bb C D Eb F = 1 2 b3 4 5 b6 b7

G Minor Pentatonic: G Bb C D F = 1 b3 4 5 b7

*Notice how the notes change within the scales.

1. Why Use the Minor Pentatonic Scale?

The appeal of the minor pentatonic scale lies in its ability to convey emotion and its ease of use across the fretboard.

- **Simplicity:** With only five notes, it is easier to learn and apply than other scales.
- **Emotional Range:** Its intervals create a sound that can range from melancholic to powerful, making it ideal for blues expression.

2. Practicing the Minor Pentatonic Scale

To become proficient with the minor pentatonic scale, regular practice in various keys and positions is essential.

- **Starting in A Minor:** Begin by practicing the scale in the key of A minor, a common key for blues guitar.
- **Different Positions:** Familiarize yourself with the scale pattern across different positions on the fretboard to improve versatility.

Practice playing the scale in multiple locations. After you have mastered it in A minor, move to G minor. Be sure to practice ascending and descending the scale to enhance visualization, finger dexterity, and memory.

3. Applying the Minor Pentatonic Scale

Once comfortable with the scale structure, begin incorporating it into your playing.

- **Improvisation:** Use the minor pentatonic scale as a basis for improvising solos, exploring different rhythms and phrasings.
- **Combining with Other Scales:** Experiment with blending the minor pentatonic scale with other scales, such as the blues scale, to expand your musical vocabulary.

By mastering the structure and application of the minor pentatonic scale, you'll gain a powerful tool for expression in your blues guitar playing.

This lesson will set the stage for further exploration of how to utilize this scale effectively across the fretboard.

Lesson 7: The 5 Magical Minor Patterns

Mastering the minor pentatonic scale in different positions across the fretboard is crucial for any blues guitarist. It allows you to play fluidly and creatively, adapting to various musical contexts with ease.

In this lesson, you'll learn how to navigate the fretboard using the minor pentatonic scale, enhancing your ability to improvise and solo.

1. Understanding the Five-Box Patterns

The minor pentatonic scale can be played in five distinct patterns, often referred to as "box patterns," across the fretboard.

Each pattern offers a unique starting point and shape, providing flexibility and variety in your playing. Since there are 5 notes in the minor pentatonic scale, you can create 5 distinct box patterns. Each one starts on a different note.

These "box" patterns are an excellent way to play the scales more easily, and a way to visualize them in your mind.

- **Pattern 1:** Begins with the root note on the 6th string and is commonly used due to its straightforward shape.
- **Pattern 2:** Shifts up the neck, starting where the 1st one left off, offering a slightly different tonal palette.
- **Pattern 3:** Continues up the neck, in the same fashion, expanding your reach and melodic options.
- **Pattern 4:** Begins with the 4th note of the scale, providing a higher register and different phrasing possibilities.
- **Pattern 5:** Starts on the 5th note of the scale, and connects back to Pattern 1.

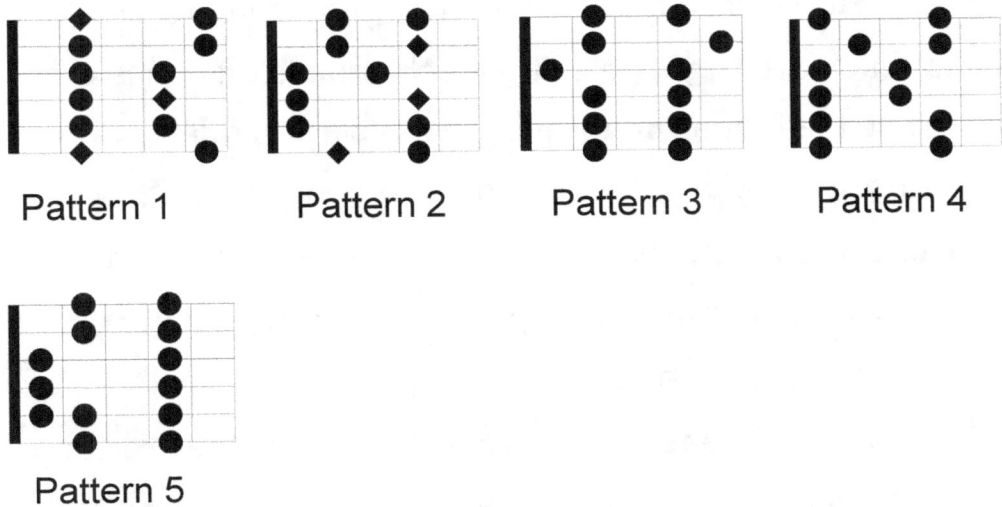

Pattern 1 Pattern 2 Pattern 3 Pattern 4

Pattern 5

*These 5 magical minor patterns create a fretboard roadmap.

Lesson 8: Exploring Expressive Techniques

Incorporating expressive techniques into your playing can transform simple notes into powerful musical statements. In this lesson, we'll explore how to use bends, slides, and hammer-ons to add emotion and depth to your minor pentatonic scales.

1. Mastering Bends for Emotion

Bending is a technique that can imbue your playing with a sense of longing or intensity, making your solos more compelling.

- **Full-Step Bends:** Practice bending the string up two frets to reach the target note. This technique is often used to mimic the human voice and adds a singing quality to your solos. Start with half-step (one fret) bends first.

- **Bend-vibrato:** These subtle bends, where the pitch is shifted slightly, and vibrated and can create tension and a unique expressive effect.

- **Bend and Release:** Bend up to a note and then release back down. This creates a dynamic movement and adds variety to your phrases.

Full-Step Bends

Bend-Vibrato

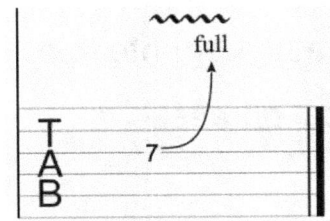

Bend-Release

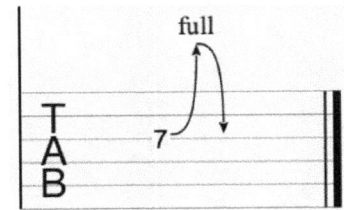

Bending guitar strings can be a bit taxing on the fingers at first, so take it easy when you're first starting. If not, you'll hate string bending. If you do, you'll learn to love the sounds that they can create.

2. Slides for Smooth Transitions

Slides can make your playing sound more fluid and connected, as if the notes are effortlessly gliding into one another.

- **Ascending Slides:** Start from a lower note and slide up to the desired note. This is excellent for building anticipation in your solos.
- **Descending Slides:** Slide down from a higher note to a lower one, often used to resolve musical phrases smoothly.
- **Slide-Vibrato:** Slide into the first note, then vibrate it, which can make your slide more dramatic.

Ascending slides

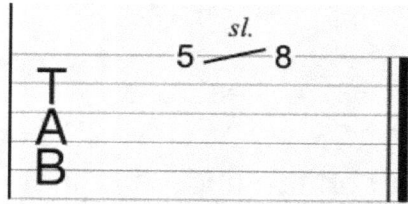

Descending slide

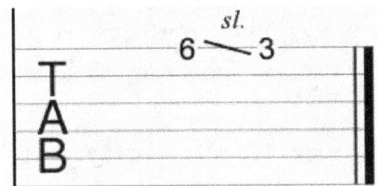

Slide-Vibrato

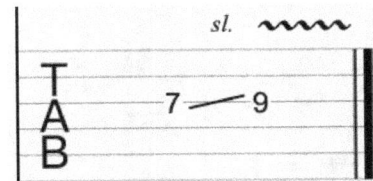

Sliding across the fret wires can be taxing on the fingers as well, especially when you're sliding over multiple ones. Start slow and increase the slide length over time.

3. Hammer-Ons, Pull-Offs for Speed and Fluidity

Hammer-ons and pull-offs allow you to play notes quickly and smoothly, enhancing the flow of your solos.

- **Single Note Hammer-Ons and Pull-Offs:** Play a note and then "hammer" your finger onto a higher fret without picking the string again. For pull-offs, play a note and pull off to the note behind it.

- **Double Hammer-Ons and Pull-Offs:** Use consecutive hammer-ons and pull-offs to create a rapid succession of notes, adding excitement and flair to your solos.
- **Hammer-On Pull-Off together:** Use the two techniques together to play three notes while only picking the first.

Hammer-Ons and Pull-Offs

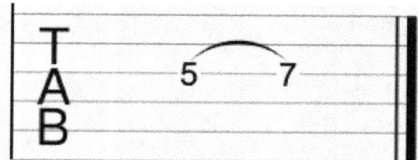 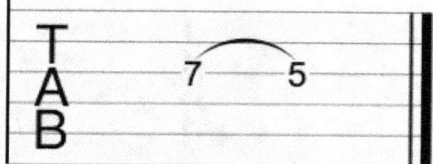

Double Hammer-Ons and Pull-offs

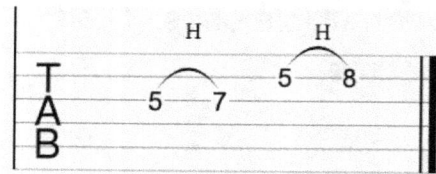 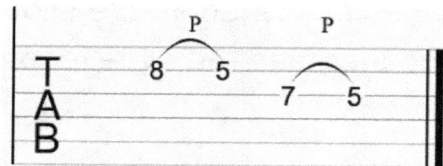

Hammer-On Pull-Off

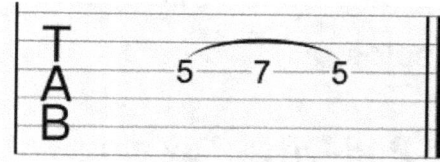

Practice these techniques individually and listen to how they make the notes sound. You will recognize them in many guitar parts of your favorite songs.

4. Combining Techniques for Maximum Expression

The real magic happens when you combine these techniques to create intricate and expressive musical phrases.

- **Bend-Release and Slide:** Bend-release a note and then slide to another, creating a seamless transition that keeps the listener engaged.
- **Hammer-On and Bend:** Use a hammer-on to quickly reach a note and then bend it, adding an element of surprise and emotion.
- **Slide and Hammer-On:** Slide into a note and immediately perform a hammer-on, which can make your playing sound more connected and lively.

These are a great way to create lead guitar licks. Put licks together, and you have phrasing, which is what we learned about earlier in the first chapter.

Bend-Release and Slide

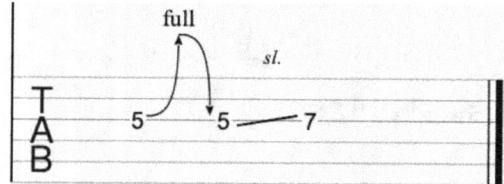

Hammer-On and Bend

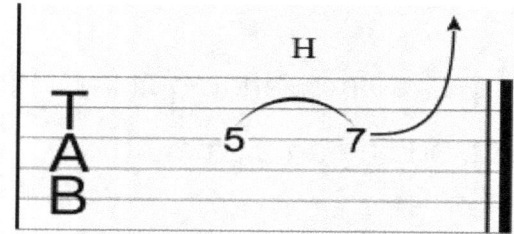

Slide and Hammer-On

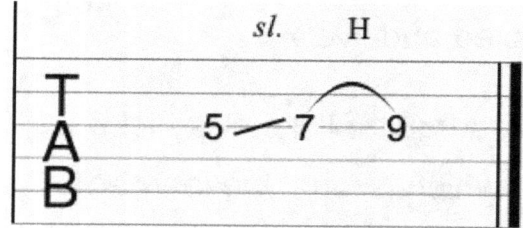

These are a great way to create lead guitar licks. Put licks together, and you have phrasing, which is what we learned about earlier in the first chapter.

5. Practice Routine for Expressive Techniques

Incorporate these techniques into your daily practice to enhance your ability to express emotion through your playing.

- **Technique Drills:** Dedicate time to practicing each technique individually, focusing on accuracy and control.
- **Combination** Exercises: Work on exercises that combine multiple techniques, allowing you to transition smoothly between them.
- **Improvisational Practice:** Use backing tracks to improvise and experiment with these techniques, discovering how they can be used to convey different emotions.

By mastering these expressive techniques, you'll be able to elevate your minor pentatonic scale playing, turning simple notes into captivating musical expressions.

This foundation will prepare you for more advanced concepts and techniques in the upcoming lessons.

Lesson 9: Improvising With the Minor Pentatonic

Improvisation is a core aspect of blues guitar playing, allowing you to express your musical ideas in the moment. This lesson will guide you through the process of using the minor pentatonic scale to develop your improvisation skills, enhancing your ability to create compelling and spontaneous solos.

1. Understanding Improvisation in Blues

Improvisation in blues is about telling a story through your guitar, using the notes and rhythms to convey emotion and connect with your audience.

- **Emotional Expression:** Focus on expressing emotion through your playing. The minor pentatonic scale provides a versatile framework for this purpose.
- **Spontaneity:** Embrace the spontaneous nature of improvisation. Allow your emotions and the music to guide you.

2. Creating Melodic Ideas

Developing strong melodic ideas is key to engaging improvisations. Start by using simple motifs and gradually expand them.

- **Motif Development:** Begin with a short, memorable motif and explore variations by altering rhythm, pitch, or dynamics.
- **Repetition and Variation:** Use repetition to reinforce your motif, while introducing variations to keep it interesting.

3. Use of Dynamics and Phrasing

Dynamics and phrasing add nuance and depth to your improvisations, allowing you to shape the musical narrative.

- **Dynamic Contrast:** Experiment with varying the volume of your playing, from soft and subtle to loud and powerful, to convey different emotions.
- **Phrasing:** Pay attention to the way you articulate each note and phrase. Use pauses and changes in rhythm to create tension and release.

4. Integrating Licks and Patterns

Incorporate licks and scale patterns into your improvisation to add structure and familiarity.

- **Blending Licks:** Mix classic blues licks with your own phrases to create a distinctive sound.
- **Pattern Exploration:** Use the five-box patterns of the minor pentatonic scale to navigate the fretboard and discover new melodic possibilities.

5. Practice Routine for Improvisation

Develop a consistent practice routine that focuses on building your improvisation skills.

- **Jam Along with Backing Tracks:** Use blues backing tracks to practice improvising in different keys and tempos. This will improve your ability to adapt to various musical settings.

By mastering improvisation with the minor pentatonic scale, you'll unlock new levels of expression and creativity in your blues guitar playing.

Lesson 10: Chapter 2 Quiz

Test your understanding of Chapter 2 by answering the following questions:

Q: What are the notes that make up the G minor scale?
A: _____

Q: What notes make up G minor pentatonic?
A: _____

Q: Why is the minor pentatonic scale so popular?
A: _____

Q: How many box patterns are there in the minor pentatonic?
A: _____

Q: Why are there only so many minor box patterns?
A: _____

Q: What does it mean to improvise with the minor pentatonic?
A: _____

Q: What role does emotional expression play in improvising?
A: _____

Chapter 2 Summary

In Chapter 2, we learned about mastering the minor pentatonic scale. A very powerful, useful tool for soloing.

First, you learned about how the minor pentatonic is a fundamental tool for guitarists used in the blues. Consisting of 5 magical notes.

Second, you learned that there are 5 magical scale patterns. These connect like puzzle pieces, span the fretboard, and allow you to build a fretboard roadmap.

Third, you learned about incorporating expressive techniques. Bends, vibrato, slides, hammer-ons, and pull-offs that allow you to create guitar licks and phrasing.

Fourth, you learned about improvising. This is where you master the scales and techniques, and let your emotions guide you without any prethought.

Fifth, you make sure you have a comprehensive understanding of the chapter with a learning assessment. This builds on your foundation and gets you ready for the next chapter.

Chapter 3 Mastering the Major Pentatonic

Lesson 11: The Major Pentatonic Scale

Understanding the differences between the major and minor pentatonic scales is crucial for any guitarist looking to master blues music. Each scale has its unique sound and application, offering distinct emotional qualities and creative possibilities.

1. Structure and Characteristics

Major Pentatonic Scale

The major pentatonic scale is derived from the major scale. It is composed of five notes, and its uplifting sound is characterized by its intervals.

- **Structure:** The major pentatonic scale consists of the root note, major second, major third, perfect fifth, and major sixth.
- **Example in C Major:** The notes are C, D, E, G, and A.
- **Sound:** This scale has a bright, happy, and open sound, often associated with positive and upbeat emotions.

2. Uses in Blues Music

Major Pentatonic in Blues

The major pentatonic scale is often used to add a brighter, more optimistic feel to blues music. It's great for solos that aim to evoke joy and energy.

- **Applications:** Use the major pentatonic scale over major chords or progressions to highlight their uplifting qualities.
- **Blues Example:** In a 12-bar blues progression, playing the major pentatonic scale over the I chord can create a refreshing contrast with the more somber tones of the minor pentatonic scale.

3. Combining Major and Minor Pentatonic Scales

A skilled blues guitarist often combines both the major and minor pentatonic scales to create dynamic and expressive solos.

- **Transitioning Between Scales:** Practice moving fluidly between the major and minor pentatonic scales to add variety and expressiveness to your music.

- **Experimentation:** Explore how the different emotional tones of each scale can complement each other, enhancing the storytelling aspect of your solos.

4. Practice Techniques

To effectively use both scales, incorporate the following practice techniques into your routine:

- **Scale Alternation:** Alternate between playing the major and minor pentatonic scales in the same key to become comfortable with their differences and transitions.
- **Improvisation Exercises:** Use backing tracks to practice improvising with both scales, discovering how each scale contributes to the overall feel of the piece.
- **Listening and Analysis:** Listen to recordings of blues guitarists who use both scales, analyzing how they blend the scales to enhance their solos.

By distinguishing between the major and minor pentatonic scales and understanding their unique qualities, you'll be prepared to utilize them effectively in your blues guitar playing.

Lesson 12: The 5 Magical Major Patterns

Understanding the major pentatonic scale patterns is crucial for any guitarist aiming to incorporate this versatile scale into their playing. Allowing you to confidently navigate the fretboard and enhance your musical expression.

Like the minors, the major pentatonic scale has five patterns, or "boxes," which can be played across the fretboard. Each pattern offers different tonal possibilities and allows you to adapt to various musical contexts.

- **Pattern 1:** Starts with the root note on the 6th string, providing a familiar shape often used for soloing.
- **Pattern 2:** Begins with the 2nd note of the scale, offering a new perspective and melodic possibilities.
- **Pattern 3:** Shifts to the 3rd note of the scale, expanding your range and melodic options.
- **Pattern 4:** Moves to the 4th note, giving access to higher register notes.
- **Pattern 5:** Starts with the 5th note, leading back into Pattern 1, completing the cycle.

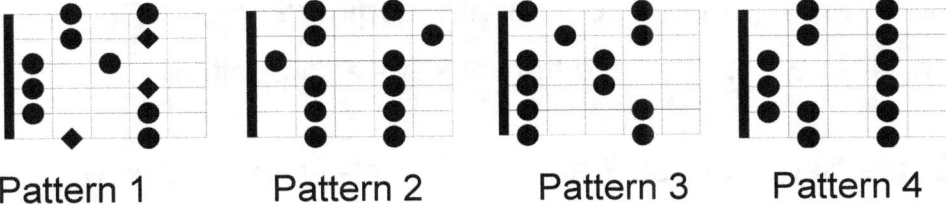

Pattern 1   Pattern 2   Pattern 3   Pattern 4

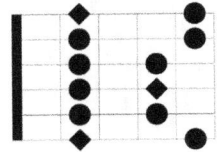

Pattern 5

Like the minors, these 5 magical patterns create a fretboard roadmap. They span from root to octave, and can be played over any major chord progression.

Their simplicity makes them easy to play and allows you to stay in key as you play them individually or move throughout them.

3. Practicing the Patterns

To master the major pentatonic scale, dedicate time to practicing these patterns in different keys and positions.

- **Scale Sequences:** Practice the scale in ascending and descending sequences, ensuring clarity and precision with each note.
- **Key Variations:** Start with the key of C major and then explore other keys like G, D, and A to increase your versatility.
- **Position Shifts:** Work on transitioning smoothly between patterns to enhance fluidity in your playing.

4. Applying Patterns in Musical Contexts

Once comfortable with the patterns, incorporate them into real musical settings to solidify your understanding of the notes and enhance your playing of the scales.

- **Soloing:** Use the patterns to craft solos that emphasize the bright, uplifting qualities of the major pentatonic scale.

- **Melodic Development:** Experiment with creating melodies and licks using different patterns to add variety and depth to your music.

- **Improvisation:** Practice improvising over backing tracks, focusing on integrating these patterns to develop your creative expression.

By familiarizing yourself with the major pentatonic scale patterns, you'll gain greater freedom and confidence in your playing.

This knowledge will serve as a foundation for exploring more advanced techniques and integrating the major pentatonic scale into your blues guitar repertoire.

Lesson 13: The Major Pentatonic in Blues

Incorporating the major pentatonic scale into your blues music opens up a world of melodic possibilities and allows you to add a brighter, more optimistic tone to your playing.

This lesson will guide you through the process of seamlessly blending the major pentatonic scale with traditional blues elements, enhancing your overall expression and creativity.

1. Understand the Role of the Pentatonics in Blues

The pentatonic scales are often used to introduce cheerful or somber tones to the blues. It can add a sense of uplift or sadness to your solos and improvisations.

- **Contrast and Balance:** By pairing the major pentatonic scale with the minor pentatonic and blues scales, you can create solos that balance emotional depth with lightheartedness.

- **Highlighting Chords:** The major pentatonic scale is particularly effective when played over major chords in a blues progression, accentuating their brighter qualities.

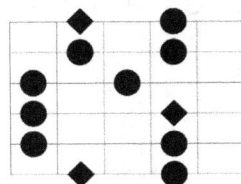

The Major Pentatonic Scale (cheerful)

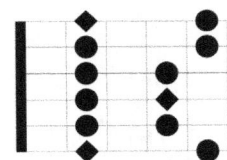

The Minor Pentatonic Scale (somber)

2. Transitioning Between Major and Minor Pentatonic Scales

To create dynamic and expressive solos, practice transitioning smoothly between the major and minor pentatonic scales. This skill allows you to shift the mood of your music effortlessly.

- **Identifying Common Notes:** Notice the shared notes between the scales to facilitate smooth transitions.
- **Phrase Development:** Begin with a phrase in the minor pentatonic scale and seamlessly integrate notes from the major pentatonic to alter the emotional impact.

3. Crafting Solos with the Major Pentatonic

When crafting solos, use the major pentatonic scale to introduce new melodies and themes that complement the blues progression.

- **Theme Variation:** Start with a simple theme using the minor pentatonic scale and modify it with major pentatonic notes to add variation and interest.
- **Creating Hooks:** Use the major pentatonic to create memorable hooks or motifs that capture the listener's attention.

4. Practical Application in Blues Progressions

Incorporate the major pentatonic scale into standard blues progressions to see how it enhances your playing.

- **12-Bar Blues:** Experiment with using the major pentatonic scale over the I chord in a 12-bar blues progression, providing a bright and lively feel.
- **Call and Response:** Implement call and response techniques using the major pentatonic scale to engage listeners and create a conversation-like dynamic in your solos.

5. Practice Routine for Integration

To effectively integrate the major pentatonic scale into your blues playing, establish a regular practice routine focused on this skill.

- **Scale Combinations:** Practice combining major and minor pentatonic scales in different keys and positions, focusing on fluid transitions.
- **Improvisation Sessions:** Dedicate time to improvising over backing tracks, emphasizing the use of the major pentatonic scale to explore its emotional range.

- **Listening and Analysis:** Listen to blues recordings that incorporate the major pentatonic scale, analyzing how experienced guitarists use it to enhance their solos.

By mastering the integration of the major pentatonic scale in your blues playing, you'll expand your musical vocabulary and enhance your ability to convey a wide range of emotions.

This lesson will empower you to create more nuanced and engaging solos, enriching your overall blues guitar repertoire.

Lesson 14: Advanced Pentatonic Techniques

In this lesson, we will delve into advanced techniques that utilize the major pentatonic scale, helping you elevate your guitar playing to new heights.

By mastering these techniques, you'll be able to infuse your solos with greater complexity, creativity, and emotional impact.

1. Incorporating Chromaticism

Chromaticism involves the use of notes outside the standard scale to create tension and interest in your solos. When you apply these chromatic notes, they can bridge the gaps between scale tones, adding a unique touch to your playing.

- **Chromatic Passing Tones:** Use chromatic notes as passing tones between two scale notes. For example, in the key of C, play C, C#, and D to create a smooth, connected line.
- **Approach Notes:** Introduce chromatic notes just before a target scale note to build anticipation and resolve tension.

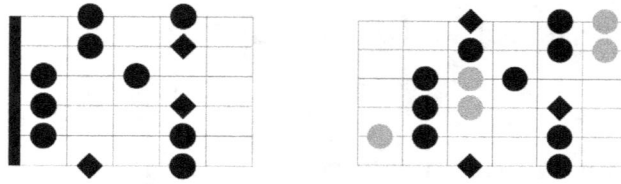

Major Pentatonic   Major Pentatonic Extended

Notice how the second example has additional notes that are next to each other. These are called chromatic notes. These notes will incorporate the flat 3rd (the blue note) and the flat 7th.

This works because the scale is still major, but with the added notes, it gives it a slightly different shade of color, with the added passing tones.

2. Utilizing Double Stops

Double stops involve playing two notes simultaneously, creating harmony and adding depth to your solos. This technique can enhance the melodic richness of the major pentatonic scale.

- **Harmonized Thirds and Sixths:** Use intervals of thirds or sixths within the scale to create pleasing harmonies. For example, play C and E together, or G and E.

- **Sliding Double Stops:** Slide into double stops to add a dynamic and expressive element to your playing.

Double Stops Within the Major Pentatonic

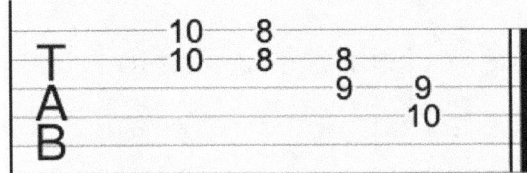

Sliding Double Stops

Remember, with double stops, you play two notes at the same time. Make sure to work on barring across two strings to get the desired effect.

3. Expanding with Extended Techniques

Extended techniques push the boundaries of traditional playing, allowing you to explore new sonic possibilities with the major pentatonic scale.

- **Tapping:** Incorporate tapping to reach higher notes quickly and add an impressive flair to your solos. Use your picking hand to tap notes beyond your fretting hand's reach.
- **Harmonics:** Use natural and artificial harmonics to add shimmering, bell-like tones. Play harmonics over the fretboard to introduce unique textures.

Finger Tapping

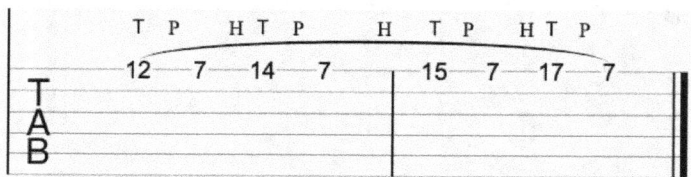

Finger tapping is a technique that utilizes both hands. Hammering on to a note with the fretboard hand, while the picking hand "taps" on another note.

This allows for a faster, smoother, but complex passage of notes. Especially when it is moved along the fretboard.

Natural Harmonics

Artificial Harmonics

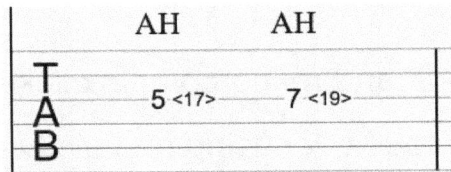

The difference between these two harmonics is the approach. Natural harmonics are when you simply tap on the fret wire. Artificial harmonics are where you use your thumb to slightly rub across the string after you pick it.

Natural harmonics are easier to produce, so I recommend starting with those. Then proceed to artificial. These produce some very cool sounds that are unlike anything else.

I recommend you study, practice, and add them to your blues guitar playing arsenal.

4. Practice Routine for Advanced Techniques

To effectively integrate these advanced techniques into your playing, establish a dedicated practice routine.

- **Technique Drills:** Spend time working on each technique individually, ensuring precision and control over each element.
- **Lick Development:** Create and refine complex licks that incorporate multiple techniques, focusing on fluidity and musicality.
- **Improvisation Sessions:** Use backing tracks to practice improvising with these techniques, exploring how they can enhance your solos.

By mastering these advanced major pentatonic techniques, you'll significantly broaden your musical palette, enabling you to deliver captivating and expressive performances.

This will prepare you for exploring even more complex musical concepts and styles in your blues guitar journey.

Lesson 15:   Chapter 3 Quiz

In this chapter, you have learned about the major pentatonic scale. This, along with the minor, will establish a solid foundation in playing the blues.

Q: What notes are in the C major scale?
A: _____

Q: How can they be used to enhance a blues solo?
A: _____

Q: What is the benefit of learning all 5 patterns?
A: _____

Q: What is the benefit of moving between the major and minor?
A: _____

Q: What is the role of pentatonic scales in the blues?
A: _____

Q: What advanced techniques can be applied to your soloing?
A: _____

Make sure to study this chapter. It will be a huge benefit to you as you progress through the blues.

Chapter 3 summary

In this chapter, you have learned about mastering the major pentatonic scale. Another powerful tool for soloing.

<u>First</u>, you learned about the structure and characteristics of the scale. Its structure, in the key of C major, and the type of characteristic sound it produces.

<u>Second</u>, you learned that, like the minor pentatonic scale, there are 5 major pentatonic scale patterns as well. These can also be used to create a fretboard roadmap.

<u>Third</u>, you learned about the role the pentatonic scales play in the blues. They can be chosen to create cheerful or somber tones of emotion.

<u>Fourth</u>, you learned about advanced techniques for soloing with the major pentatonic. Techniques such as chromatic notes, double stops, finger tapping, and harmonics.

<u>Fifth</u>, you are presented with another learning assessment to make sure you fully understand the material. This builds another brick in your blues guitar foundation.

Chapter 4 Unlocking the Blues Scales

Lesson 16: Uniqueness of the Blues Scale

The blues scale is a cornerstone of blues music, characterized by its distinct sound that captures the essence of the genre. Understanding what makes the blues scale unique is crucial for any guitarist looking to master blues playing.

1. The Structure of the Blues Scale

The blues scale is a variation of the pentatonic scale, distinguished by the inclusion of the "blue" note, which gives it its signature sound.

In the major blues scale, the "blue" note that is added will be the flat 3rd. Let's look at an example in the key of C major, as we did with the major pentatonic.

C Major Scale: C D E F G A B = 1 2 3 4 5 6 7

C Major Pentatonic: C D E G A = 1 2 3 5 6

C Major Blues Scale: C D Eb E G A = 1 2 b3 3 5 6

- **Notes in the Blues Scale:** The blues scale consists of six notes. In the key of A minor pentatonic, for example, these notes are A, C, D, Eb, E, and G.
- **The Blue Note:** The Eb is the blue note, adding a sense of tension and emotional depth that is quintessential to the blues.

A Minor Scale: A B C D E F G = 1 2 3 4 5 6 7

A Minor Pentatonic: A C D E G = 1 3 4 5 7

A Minor Blues Scale: A C D Eb E G = 1 3 4 b5 5 7

As you can see from the examples presented, this "blue" note works with both the major and minor pentatonic scales. This is good because it allows you to extend your scale vocabulary.

Major Blues   Minor Blues

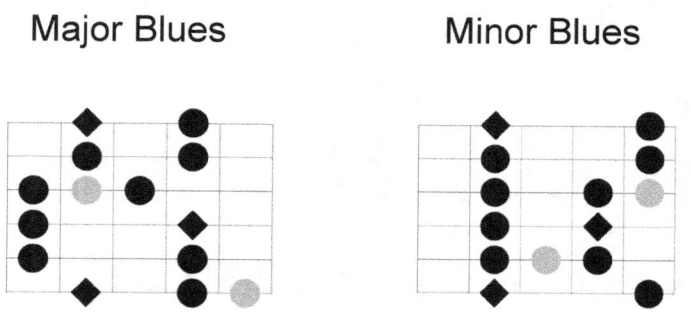

Flat 3rd note added   Flat 5th note added

2. Emotional Expression

The unique structure of the blues scale allows for a wide range of emotional expression, making it ideal for conveying the raw, heartfelt emotions that define blues music.

- **Tension and Release:** The inclusion of the blue note introduces tension, which can be resolved by moving to the surrounding notes. This tension and release create a dynamic emotional experience.
- **Soulful Sound:** The blues scale's intervals produce a sound that is both soulful and evocative, capable of expressing feelings of longing, sadness, and resilience.

3. Versatility in Music

While the blues scale is a staple of blues music, its versatility makes it applicable across genres such as rock, jazz, and even pop.

- **Adaptability:** The scale's structure allows it to be easily adapted to different musical contexts, making it a valuable tool for improvisation and soloing beyond the blues.

- **Cross-Genre Appeal:** Many iconic rock and jazz solos incorporate the blues scale, demonstrating its widespread influence and appeal.

4. Application in Blues Solos

The blues scale is a fundamental tool for crafting expressive and engaging solos, allowing guitarists to tap into the emotional depth of the blues.

- **Solo Construction:** Use the blues scale as a foundation for building solos that capture the essence of the blues. Focus on incorporating the blue note to add emotional intensity.
- **Improvisation:** The scale provides a framework for spontaneous solos, enabling guitarists to create solos that resonate with audiences.

By understanding what makes the blues scale unique, you'll gain a deeper appreciation for its role in blues music and its potential for emotional expression. Mastering the blues scale will empower you to create solos that are rich in feeling.

Lesson 17: Blues Scales Patterns Across the Neck

1. Five Pattern Overview

Since the blues scales are extensions of the pentatonic scales, they too can be broken down into the five distinct patterns.

The 5 Major Blues Scales

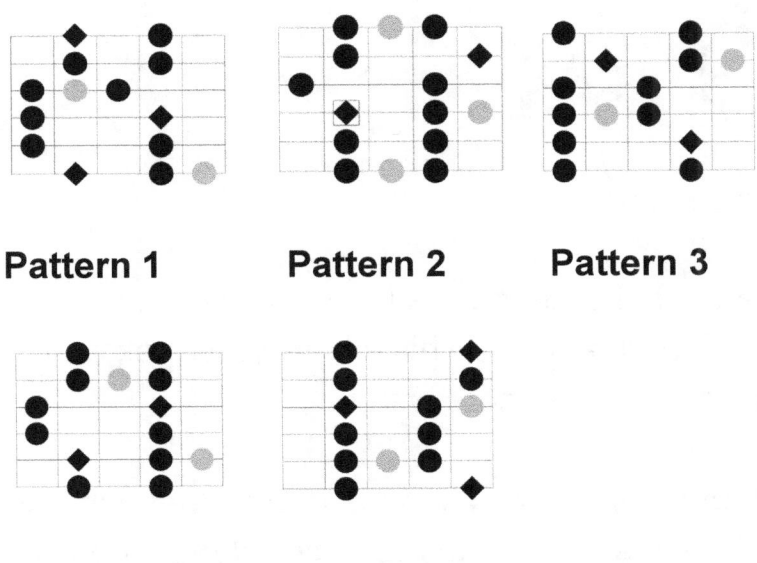

Pattern 1   Pattern 2   Pattern 3

Pattern 4   Pattern 5

As you can clearly see, these are the same as the major pentatonics, with just the flat 3rd note added.

The 5 Minor Blues Scales

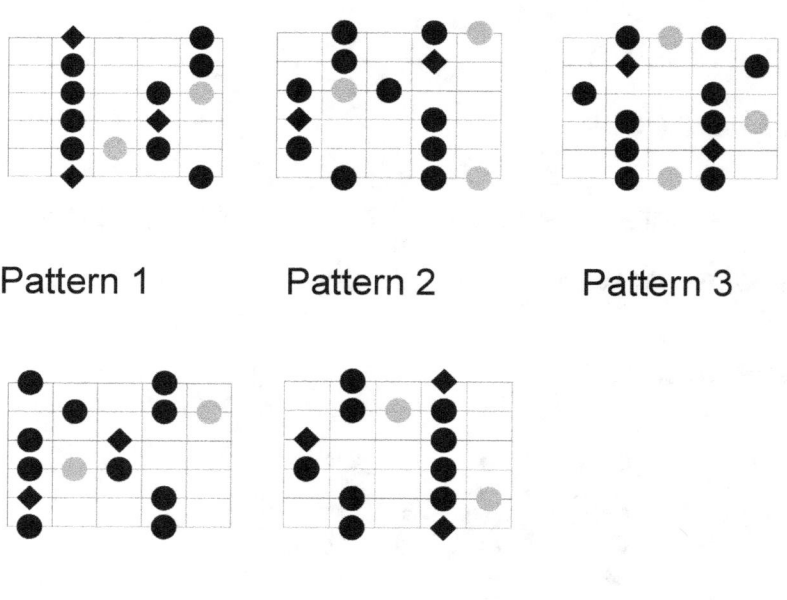

Pattern 1   Pattern 2   Pattern 3

Pattern 4   Pattern 5

Once again, you can see that these are the minor pentatonic scales with the flat 5th note added. This allows you to extend the pentatonic scale and create more with it.

Remember, no matter what key you choose to play these in, the flat 3rd will always be added to create the major blues, and the flat 5th will be added to create the minor blues.

2. Practicing Transitions Between Patterns

To achieve fluidity and coherence in your solos, practice transitioning smoothly between these patterns. This skill allows you to connect ideas seamlessly and maintain musical flow.

- **Linking Patterns:** Work on moving from one pattern to the next without pausing, focusing on the connection points where one pattern leads into another.
- **Position Shifts:** Practice sliding or jumping between patterns, which adds dynamic movement to your solos.

Linking patterns

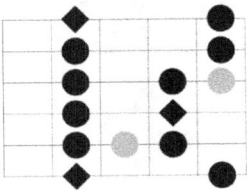

Minor Blues Scale Pattern 1

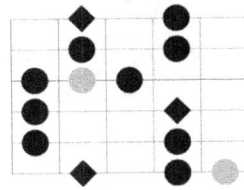

Major Blues Scale Pattern 1

Work on moving between these two patterns seamlessly.

Position Shifts

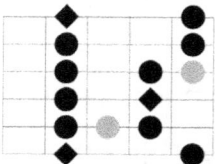

Minor Blues Scale Pattern 1

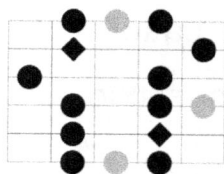

Minor Blues Scale pattern 3

Practice sliding or jumping between these two scale patterns, as well as ones in the major blues. This approach will not only help you to master the individual scale patterns, but it will also help with fretboard mastery.

3. Exercises for Fretboard Familiarity

Developing a deep understanding of the fretboard is key to mastering the blues scale. Regular exercises can help reinforce your familiarity with the scale patterns.

- **Scale Runs:** Practice ascending and descending scale runs using all five patterns, ensuring each note is clear and precise.
- **Pattern Combinations:** Combine different patterns within a single exercise to challenge your ability to navigate the fretboard efficiently.
- **Improvisational Drills:** Set aside time to improvise freely using the blues scale, focusing on utilizing multiple patterns to create varied and interesting solos.
- **Backing Tracks:** Play along with blues backing tracks, using different patterns to explore how they fit within various chord changes.
- **Jam Sessions:** Engage in jam sessions with other musicians, applying your knowledge of the blues scale to contribute creatively.

By practicing this lesson, you should feel confident playing the blues scale across the entire fretboard. Using all five patterns will enhance your improvisation and soloing capabilities. This skill will serve as a way to keep building your foundation.

Lesson 18: Combining Scales for Blues Solos

Blending different scales in your solos is a powerful technique that can add depth and variety to your blues playing. Allowing you to focus on how to effectively combine scales can create expressive and dynamic solos.

1. Understanding the Role of Scale Combinations

Combining scales allows you to explore a wider range of notes and emotional expressions in your solos. This technique can introduce new textures and moods, making your music more engaging and nuanced.

- **Emotional Range:** By switching between scales, you can convey different emotions, from the soulful and melancholic tones of the minor pentatonic scale to the uplifting brightness of the major pentatonic scale.
- **Dynamic Solos:** Mixing scales can add contrast and interest to your solos, keeping the listener engaged and enhancing the storytelling aspect of your music.

2. Blending the Blues Scale with Pentatonic Scales

The blues scale, with its unique blue note, can be seamlessly combined with both the major and minor pentatonic scales to expand your musical palette.

- **Combining with Minor Pentatonic:** Use the blues scale to add tension and color to the minor pentatonic scale. The blue note (Eb in the key of A minor) can create a striking contrast that enhances the emotional impact of your solos.
- **Integrating Major Pentatonic:** Mix the blues scale with the major pentatonic scale to introduce a brighter feel. This combination is particularly effective for solos that aim to balance soulful expression with a sense of joy or optimism.

3. Techniques for Smooth Transitions

To effectively blend scales, practice techniques that facilitate smooth transitions between them, ensuring your solos remain cohesive and fluid.

- **Identify Common Notes:** Understanding the shared notes between scales can help you transition more naturally. For instance, in the key of A, the notes A, C, and E are common to both the blues and minor pentatonic scales.
- **Phrase Overlap:** Start a phrase in one scale and subtly shift to another by overlapping notes. This approach maintains continuity while introducing new scale tones.

4. Creating Melodic Interest

Blending scales can lead to more interesting and varied melodies. Use this technique to develop solos that captivate your audience.

- **Motif Development:** Craft motifs that incorporate notes from different scales. This can add complexity and richness to your solos.
- **Rhythmic Variations:** Experiment with different rhythms when transitioning between scales to emphasize certain notes or phrases, adding a dynamic element to your playing.

5. Practice Routine for Scale Blending

To master the art of combining scales, incorporate the following exercises into your practice routine:

- **Scale Alternation Exercises:** Practice alternating between scales in the same key, focusing on smooth transitions and melodic continuity.
- **Improvisation Over Backing Tracks:** Use blues backing tracks to practice improvising with combined scales, exploring how each scale influences the overall mood and feel of your solos.
- **Listening and Analysis:** Study recordings of blues guitarists who adeptly blend scales, paying attention to how they navigate transitions and create contrast in their solos.

By mastering the ability to combine scales in your solos, you'll unlock new levels of creativity and expression in your blues guitar playing. Provide you with the tools to craft dynamic and emotionally resonant storytelling solos,

Lesson 19: Creating Additional Emotional Impact

One of the most compelling aspects of blues music is its ability to convey deep emotions through guitar playing. The blues scale, with its distinctive sound and expressive potential, is an essential tool for achieving this emotional impact.

In this lesson, we'll continue to explore techniques for using the blues scale to express emotion and connect with your audience on a deeper level. You can never have too many tools in your toolbox for this concept.

1. Understanding Emotional Expression in Blues

Blues music is renowned for its emotional depth, often reflecting themes of longing, heartache, and resilience. To convey these emotions effectively, it's essential to focus on how you play, not just what you play.

- **Feel the Music:** Allow yourself to be moved by the music. The more you connect emotionally with the piece, the more your audience will feel it too.

- **Authenticity:** Express genuine emotions through your playing. Authenticity resonates with listeners and makes your music more compelling.

2. Emphasizing the Blue Note

The blue note is the heart of the blues scale, adding tension and emotional richness to your music. Understanding how to use it effectively can elevate your playing.

- **Highlighting Tension:** Use the blue note (Eb in the key of A minor) to create tension within your solos. This tension can be resolved by moving to adjacent notes, creating an emotional journey.
- **Targeting the Blue Note:** Emphasize the blue note in key phrases to add intensity and expressiveness. This can be done through techniques like bends or vibrato, which make the note stand out.

3. Phrasing for Emotional Impact

Phrasing is the art of organizing musical ideas into meaningful and expressive statements. In blues, phrasing plays a crucial role in conveying emotion.

- **Use of Space:** Silence between notes can be as powerful as the notes themselves. Use pauses to build anticipation and highlight key moments in your solos.
- **Dynamic Variation:** Vary the volume and intensity of your playing to reflect different emotions. Soft, subtle passages can convey introspection, while louder, more aggressive phrases can express passion or frustration.

By mastering the use of the blues scale to create emotional impact, you'll enhance your ability to connect with your audience and deliver powerful, moving performances.

Preparing you for further exploration of playing techniques in the upcoming chapters, and adding another brick to your foundation.

Remember, the more solid your foundation, the more solid your guitar playing. So don't skip over these lessons.

Lesson 20: Chapter 4 Quiz

Answer these questions to make sure you fully understand the lessons presented in it.

Q: What type of note creates the blues scale?

A: _____

Q: What is the structure of the major blues scale?

A: _____

Q: How does the blues scale allow a wider range of soloing?

A: _____

Q: How many blues scale patterns are there?

A: _____

Q: What is the benefit of knowing all of them?

A: _____

Q: How can emphasizing the "blue" note enhance a solo?

A: _____

Q: What two techniques can convey deep emotion in a solo?

A: _____

Chapter 4 Summary

In chapter four, you have learned how the blues scale is the cornerstone of blues music. Understanding what makes the blues scale unique is crucial for any mastering the blues.

First, you learned how the blues scale's distinct sound captures the essence of this style of music. This is due to the addition of the "blue" note.

Second, you learned about the 5 blues scale patterns and how they are an extension of the pentatonic scale. This is done by adding the "blue" note in both major and minor.

Third, you learned about combining scales to explore a wider range of dynamics and expression in your solos. This will also help you to improve your mastery of the fretboard.

Fourth, you learn about exploring additional techniques to create emotion. Allowing you to develop a deeper connection with your audience.

Fifth, you have once again been presented with a learning assessment. This allows you to add a few more bricks to building your foundation.

Chapter 5 Phrasing with the Blues Scales

Lesson 21: Bending and Vibrato Techniques

In this lesson, we'll explore famous phrasing techniques such as bending and vibrato. These will perfect your dynamics and enhance the landscape of your solos.

Mastering bending and vibrato is essential for any blues guitarist seeking to achieve a soulful and expressive sound. These techniques can transform a simple note into a powerful emotional statement.

1. Understanding Bending

Bending is a hallmark of blues guitar, allowing you to mimic the expressive qualities of the human voice. By precisely controlling the pitch of a note, you can add emotion and depth to your solos.

But for that to happen, you must put in the work. Start slow, bend slightly, and as your fingers build strength over time, gradually increase the length of the bent note.

- **Full-Step Bends:** Practice bending the string up a full step (two frets) to reach the target note. This technique is often used to create a vocal-like quality, adding a sense of longing or intensity.
- **Pre-Bend and Release:** Bend the string to the desired pitch before striking it, then release it back to the original pitch. This technique adds dynamic movement to your playing and can create a sense of tension and release.

Full-Step Bends

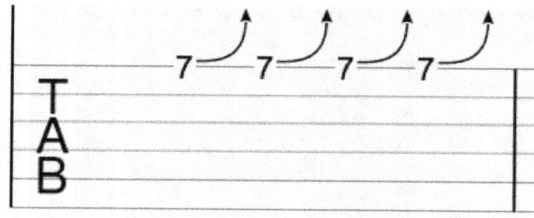

Bend and Release

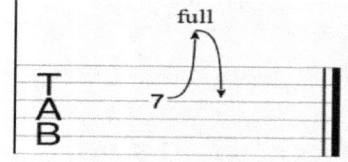

Practice these techniques daily to strengthen your fingers. I recommend using lighter strings as they will be easier to bend.

2. Developing Vibrato

Vibrato involves varying the pitch of a sustained note, adding richness and character. A well-executed vibrato can make your notes sing, adding a layer of expressiveness to your playing.

- **Wrist Vibrato:** Use your wrist to rock the string back and forth gently, creating a smooth and controlled vibrato. This method is often favored for its consistency and ease of control.
- **Finger Vibrato:** Employ your fingers to create vibrato, which can offer a more nuanced and personal touch. This technique involves moving your finger quickly along the string while maintaining contact with the fretboard.
- **Wide vs. Narrow Vibrato:** Experiment with the width of your vibrato, from narrow (subtle pitch variation) to wide (more pronounced pitch changes), to convey different emotions.

Vibrato is a technique that is very personal, and everyone does it a little differently. As you progress in your studies, you'll develop your own style.

Vibrato Examples

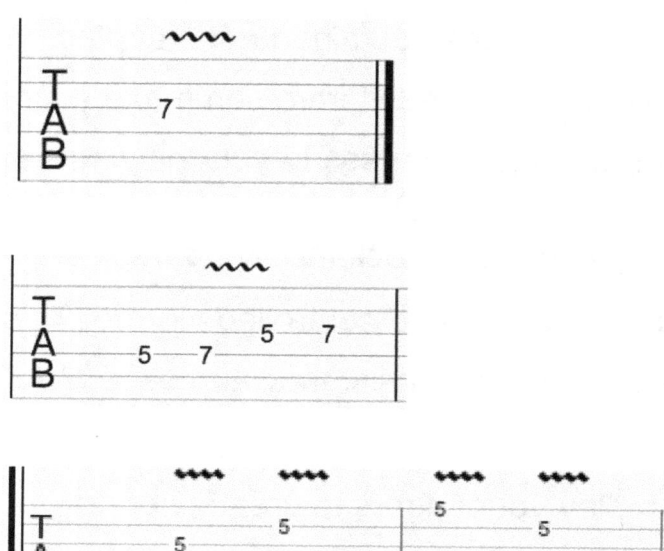

Practice these daily to develop this technique. The goal is to make the note sound like a singer holding a note, vibrating their vocal cords.

This is a very personal technique and will take some time to master. Just take it easy when first starting. As time goes on, you'll get better and better.

3. Combining Bending and Vibrato

The combination of bending and vibrato can elevate your playing, allowing for a seamless blend of pitch and expression.

- **Bend and Hold with Vibrato:** After bending a note, hold the pitch and apply vibrato for a singing, emotional effect. This technique is powerful for emphasizing key notes in your solos.
- **Bend-Release Vibrato:** Apply vibrato to a bent and released note to maintain its expressive quality and add a dynamic twist to your phrases.
- **Repeated Bend Vibrato:** This is where you continue to express the same thing over and over again to create tension.

Bends and Hold with Vibrato

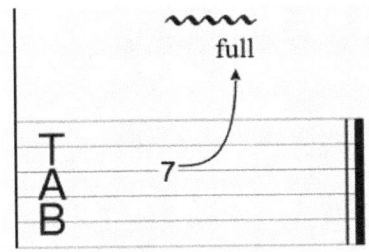

Bend-Release Vibrato

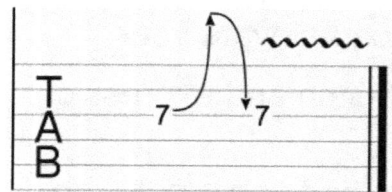

Repeated Bend Vibrato

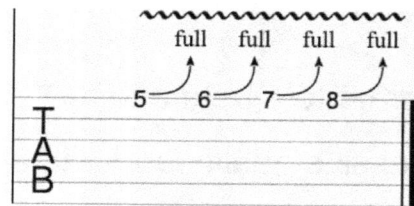

Use light strings (not too light), and it will make bending strings easier. I use 9-42. A very common guitar string gauge.

4. Practice Routine for Bending and Vibrato

To perfect these techniques, integrate focused daily practice sessions into your routine. This will keep them sharp and working as they should when you need them.

- **Precision Drills:** Work on bending to the correct pitch by using a tuner to ensure accuracy. Practice bending and holding the note without wavering.
- **Vibrato Exercises:** Spend time developing a consistent vibrato. Focus on maintaining a steady motion and experiment with different speeds and widths.
- **Combination Practice:** Combine bending and vibrato in your practice sessions to develop fluidity and expression. Use backing tracks to apply these techniques in a musical context.

5. Additional Musical Concepts

Once comfortable with bending and vibrato, apply these techniques to your blues playing to enhance your musical expression.

- **Master bending and vibrato:** You'll unlock new levels of emotional expression in your blues guitar playing.
- **Increase your foundation:** This will prepare you for exploring additional expressive techniques in the subsequent lessons.

Add these techniques as an addition to your practice routine.

Lesson 22: Sliding, Hammer-ons and Pull-offs

Incorporating slides and hammer-ons/pull-offs into your playing can significantly enhance the fluidity and expressiveness of your blues guitar solos.

These techniques allow you to create seamless transitions between notes, adding a lyrical quality to your music. Learn how these techniques effectively enrich your blues playing.

1. Mastering Slides

Slides are a powerful technique for creating smooth, connected lines in your solos. By gliding from one note to another, you can add a sense of continuity and motion to your playing.

- **Sliding Up:** Begin by playing a note and sliding up to a higher note. This technique is often used to build tension or anticipation.
- **Sliding Down:** Start with a higher note and slide down to a lower one, which can be used to resolve phrases or create a sense of conclusion.
- **Sliding Up and Down:** Use slides to move up and down in a phrase, adding drama and flair to your entrance.

Sliding Up

Sliding Down

Sliding Up and Down

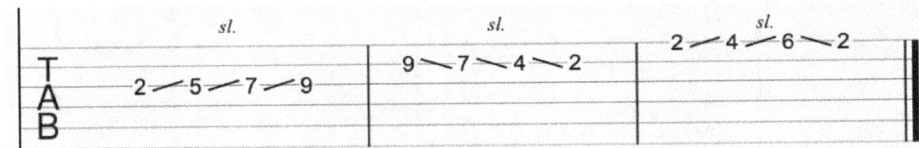

Work on these daily to build finger strength and accuracy in sliding from note to note.

2. Understanding Hammer-ons and Pull-offs

Hammer-ons and pull-offs are essential for playing notes quickly and smoothly without picking each one. These techniques add speed and fluidity, making your solos sound more intricate and connected.

- **Hammer-On:** Play a note and then "hammer" your finger onto a higher fret without picking the string again.
- **Pull-Off:** Begin with your finger on a higher fret, play the note, and then pull your finger off to let a lower note ring.
- **Combination:** Use hammer-ons and pull-offs in succession to create fast, flowing passages.

Hammer-On

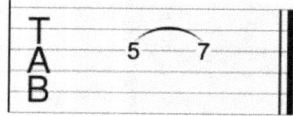

Pull-Off

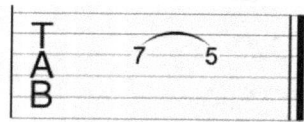

Hammer-On Pull-Off

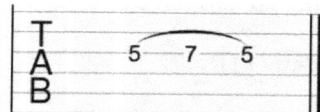

These are the essence of guitar solos and melody lines.

3. Techniques for Fluid Transitions

Combining slides, hammer-ons, and pull-offs can lead to incredibly fluid soloing. Practice these techniques to achieve seamless transitions between notes.

- **Phrase Linking:** Use slides to connect different sections of a solo, ensuring each phrase flows naturally into the next.
- **Speed and Precision:** Focus on executing hammer-ons and pull-offs with speed and accuracy, maintaining clarity and control in your playing.

4. Practice Routine for These Techniques

To master these techniques, incorporate the following exercises into your practice routine:

- **Scale Sequences:** Practice sliding, hammer-ons, and pull-offs within scale patterns to improve dexterity and fluidity.

- **Phrase Development:** Create phrases that combine these techniques, ensuring transitions are smooth and expressive.
- **Improvisational Drills:** Use backing tracks to apply slides and hammer-ons/pull-offs in a musical context, experimenting with how they can enhance your solos.

By mastering sliding and hammer-on/pull-off techniques, you'll enhance the fluidity and expressiveness of your blues guitar solos, enabling you to create captivating and seamless musical statements.

It is highly recommended that you practice these daily, as they will set up your foundation for blues guitar soloing. They will also prepare you for exploring additional expressive techniques in the upcoming lessons.

Lesson 23: Dynamics in Phrasing The Blues

Exploring the nuances of dynamics and phrasing is essential for any blues guitarist aiming to create expressive and impactful music.

Understanding Dynamics in Blues

Dynamics refer to the variations in loudness and softness in your playing. Mastering dynamics can help you convey emotion and keep your audience engaged.

- **Volume Variation:** Use changes in volume to emphasize different parts of your solo. Louder sections can convey excitement or intensity, while softer passages can evoke introspection or vulnerability.
- **Crescendo and Decrescendo:** Gradually increase (crescendo) or decrease (decrescendo) the volume within phrases to create a sense of movement and tension.
- **Accentuation:** Accentuate specific notes or chords to highlight key moments in your music. This can draw attention to important phrases and add emphasis.

Phrasing for Expressiveness

Phrasing is the way you group and articulate notes to create musical sentences. It plays a crucial role in conveying emotion and storytelling in blues.

- **Call and Response:** This technique involves playing a musical "call" followed by a "response," mimicking a conversation. It adds a dynamic, interactive element to your solos.
- **Use of Space:** Silence is as important as sound in phrasing. Use pauses to create anticipation and make your phrases more impactful.
- **Rhythmic Variation:** Experiment with different rhythms within your phrases to add interest and complexity. Syncopation and off-beats can create a more engaging and unpredictable sound.

Combining Dynamics and Phrasing

Integrating dynamics and phrasing allows you to craft solos that are both technically proficient and emotionally resonant.

- **Volume Control:** Practice playing scales and licks at varying volumes, focusing on smooth transitions between dynamic levels.
- **Phrase Creation:** Develop phrases that incorporate dynamic changes and varied rhythms. Experiment with different phrasing techniques to explore their expressive potential.
- **Improvisational** Practice: Use backing tracks to apply dynamics and phrasing in a musical context, focusing on how these elements can enhance your solos.
- **Lyrical Phrasing:** Incorporate these techniques into your phrasing to create musical lines that resonate with the qualities of a vocal performance.

Utilizing dynamics and phrasing in your playing, you'll unlock new levels of expression in your blues guitar solos. This will allow you to deliver performances that are both powerful and moving.

But as with all other techniques, you must put into application what you have learned. You must be diligent in your studies and develop discipline in your practice sessions.

Lesson 24: Developing Your Unique Blues Style

Creating a unique blues style is an exciting journey that allows you to express your personality and emotions through your guitar playing. This lesson will guide you through the process of combining various techniques to craft your individual sound and stand out as a blues guitarist.

1. Embrace Your Influences

Every guitarist is influenced by the music they love. Embrace these influences to help shape your unique style while ensuring you add your own touch.

- **Identify Inspirations:** Make a list of your favorite blues musicians and analyze what elements of their playing resonate with you.
- **Borrow and Adapt:** Incorporate techniques, phrasing, or licks from these artists into your playing, while adapting them to fit your style.

By taking this approach, you will also help yourself to recognize these concepts and techniques when you hear them in songs.

2. Experiment with Techniques

Exploring different techniques will allow you to discover new sounds and expand your musical vocabulary.

- **Technique Exploration:** Experiment with bending, vibrato, slides, hammer-ons, and pull-offs to see how they can enhance your sound.
- **Mix and Match:** Combine techniques in unconventional ways to create fresh and interesting musical phrases.

3. Crafting Your Sound

Your tone is an integral part of your unique style. Experiment with your instrument and equipment to find a sound that reflects your personality.

- **Guitar and Gear Settings:** Play around with your guitar's tone controls and amplifier settings to find a sound that feels authentic to you.
- **Effects and Pedals:** Explore different effects pedals, such as overdrive, reverb, or delay, to add texture and depth to your playing.

4. Developing Signature Licks

Creating signature licks can help define your style and make your playing instantly recognizable.

- **Original Licks:** Start by modifying existing licks or creating entirely new ones that highlight your strengths and preferences.
- **Consistent Elements:** Include consistent elements, such as rhythmic patterns or specific notes, in your licks to make them uniquely yours.

5. Expressive Playing

To make your style stand out, focus on expressing emotion through your playing. This connection with the audience is what makes blues music so powerful.

- **Emotional Focus:** Concentrate on conveying emotions through dynamics, phrasing, and note choice.
- **Storytelling:** Think of your solos as stories, using musical phrases to express a narrative that captivates your listeners.

*Remember, music is all about emotion!

6. Practice Routine for Style Development

To cultivate your unique style, incorporate dedicated practice sessions into your routine.

- **Style Exploration:** Dedicate time to exploring different techniques and experimenting with your sound.
- **Recording and Reflection:** Record your practice sessions and listen back to identify unique elements you can develop further.
- **Improvisational Practice:** Use backing tracks to practice improvising, allowing your style to evolve naturally as you explore new ideas.

7. Showcasing Your Style

Once you've developed your unique blues style, look for opportunities to showcase it.

- **Live Performances:** Participate in open mic nights or jam sessions to share your sound with others.
- **Online Platforms:** Share recordings or videos of your playing on social media or music platforms to reach a wider audience.

By combining various techniques and embracing your influences, you'll develop a unique blues style that reflects your individuality as a guitarist.

This lesson has given you ideas that can empower you to express your musical identity and create a lasting impact in the blues genre.

Make sure to master the technical skills discussed in this training course. Develop patience, as not all things will come easily. Work diligently on the things that need more work, and celebrate your victories.

All this and more can help you to develop your own style of playing. That is what's fun about playing the guitar. Everything can be personalized to fit you and what you stand for.

Through daily study and practice, you will build enough confidence to step out and show the world who you are. When you do, all the hard work and work put in will allow you to shine and make people say, "Wow, that's amazing!"

Lesson 25: Chapter 5 Quiz

In this chapter, you have learned techniques for expressive blues playing. Ways to develop a sound unique to you.

Q: What is the purpose of bending notes in blues soloing?

A: _____

Q: How can using vibrato express the note you are playing?

A: _____

Q: How can slides enhance the notes in a blues solo?

A: _____

Q: Why are hammer-ons and pull-offs so beneficial to soloing?

A: _____

Q: What is the role of dynamics and the emotional impact?

A: _____

Q: What step can be taken to develop your own style?

A: _____

Q: What builds the most self-confidence in learning the guitar?

A: _____

Chapter 5 Summary

In this chapter, we have learned about phrasing with the blues scale. Exploring famous phrasing techniques such as bending and vibrato. Mastering these techniques and those like them is essential for you to craft engaging, memorable solos.

First, you learned about bending and vibrato techniques. These are the foundations of guitar solos. Manipulating the strings in a way, they convey your mastery over the instrument.

Second, you learned about slides, hammer-ons, and pull-offs. These are also fundamental techniques needed to create riffs, solos, and amazing melody lines.

Third, you learned about dynamic phrasing in the blues. This is where you add emotion to your musical statement. Where your articulation notes paint a beautiful musical landscape.

Fourth, you learned about ways you can develop your own musical style. This is the ultimate goal. To put your own personal point of view on the music world.

Fifth, you are once again presented with a chapter learning assessment. This is a great way to test that you know the material thoroughly and are ready for the next step.

Chapter 6 Rhythm progressions in Blues

Lesson 26: Common Blues Progressions

Understanding and mastering common blues chord progressions is fundamental for any guitarist seeking to delve into the heart of blues music.

These progressions provide the backbone of countless blues songs and are essential for both rhythm playing and soloing.

1. The 12-Bar Blues Progression

The 12-bar blues progression is the most iconic and widely used chord progression in blues music. It forms the structure of many classic blues songs and provides a solid foundation for improvisation and soloing.

- **Structure:** The 12-bar blues progression typically follows a pattern of three four-bar phrases, using three primary chords: the I, IV, and V chords.

*Hundreds of songs have been created with this combo!

The 12-bar blues in the key of C major would be:

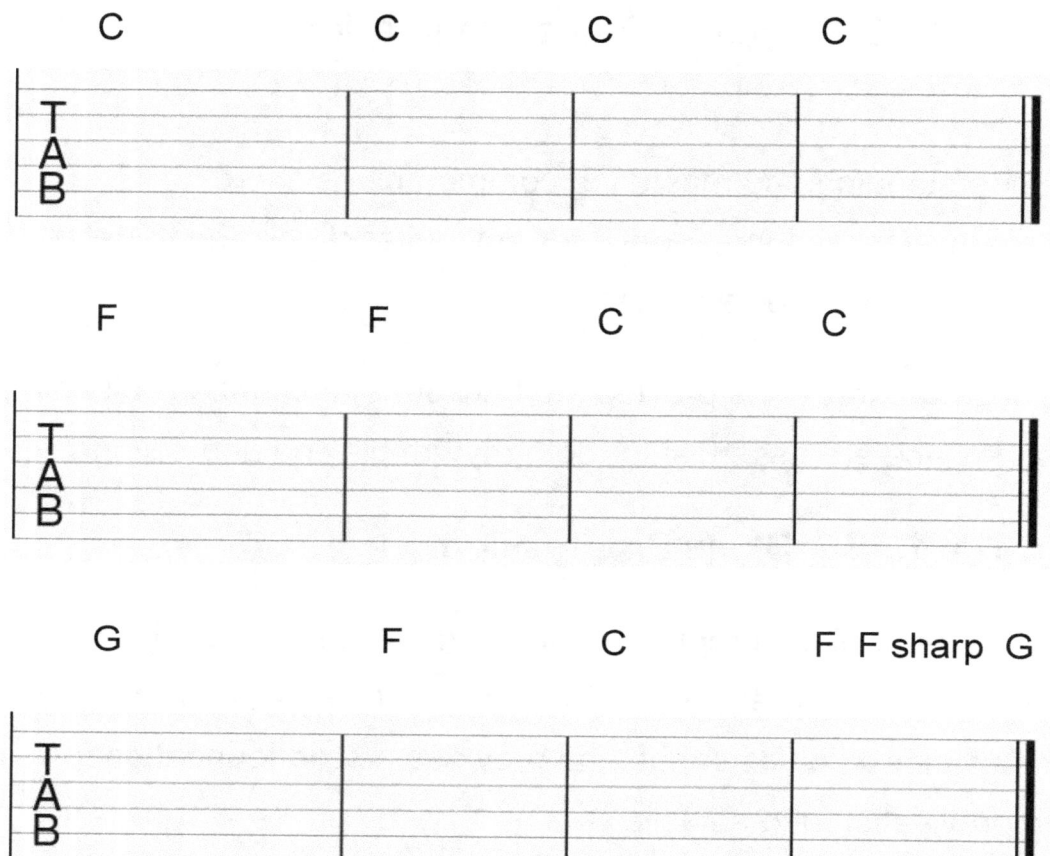

The last measure incorporates the F sharp chord for what is called a turnaround. This brings you back to the start, allowing you to continue without a break in the progression.

Let's now look at a couple of variations of this progression.

2. 8-Bar Blues Progression

The 8-bar blues progression is a shorter alternative to the 12-bar format, often used in faster or more upbeat blues songs.

- **Structure:** This progression typically involves two four-bar phrases.
  - ○ **Example in Key of A:** A - D - A - A, D - D - A - E

As you can see, these reside over 8 bars of music. Instead of the 12 bars from the last example.

3. 16-Bar Blues Progression

The 16-bar blues progression in A

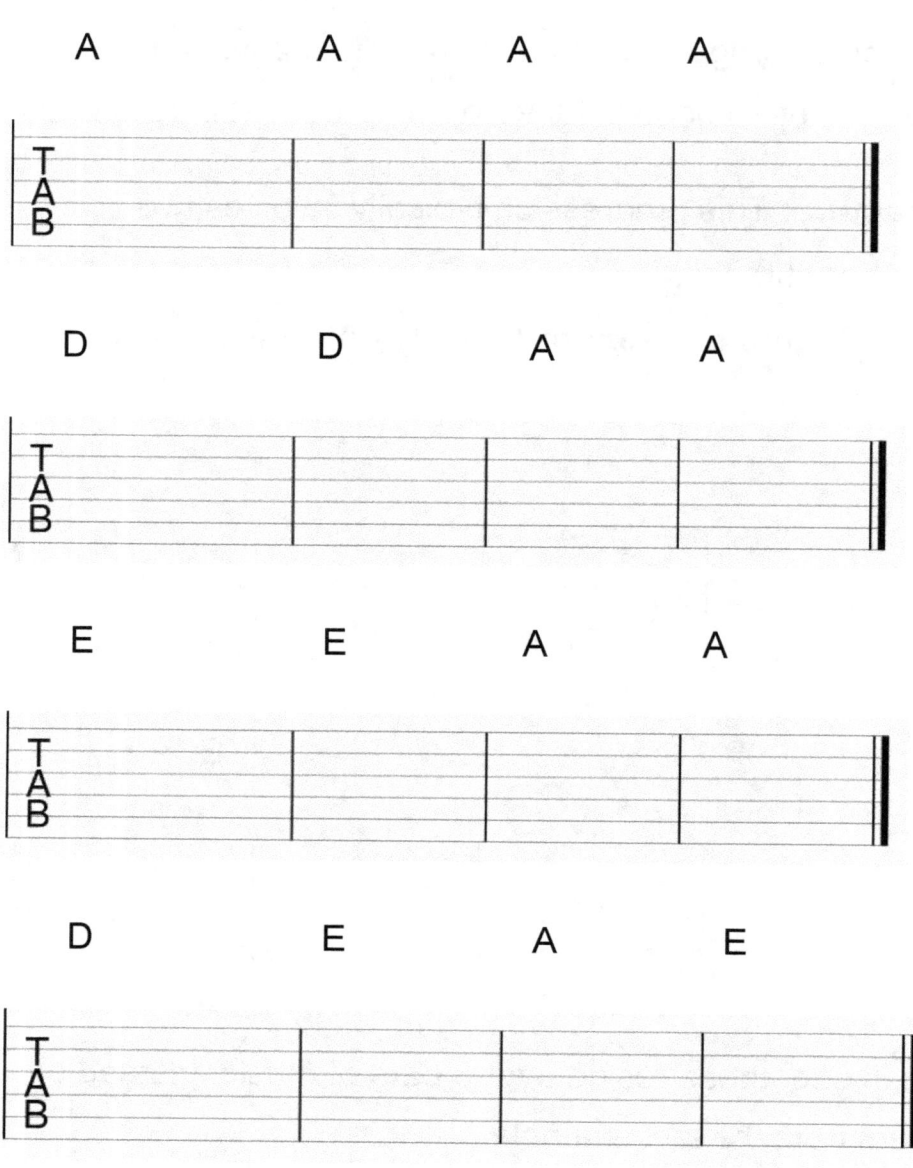

4. Applying Chord Progressions in Blues Playing

Understanding these chord progressions allows you to play and compose blues music confidently. Here's how to apply them:

- **Rhythm Playing:** Practice playing these progressions with different strumming patterns and tempos to develop your rhythm skills.
- **Soloing:** Use these progressions as a foundation for improvisation, applying scales and licks to create expressive solos.

By mastering these common blues chord progressions, and once you like it, you'll gain a deeper understanding of blues music rhythm.

This will allow you to enhance your ability to create and play blues solos that capture the emotion of your audience.

The better your understanding of rhythm and rhythm concepts, the more you'll shine when playing jaw-dropping solos.

Lesson 27: Rhythm and Timing in the Blues

Mastering rhythm and timing is crucial for any blues guitarist. These elements form the backbone of blues music, giving it its distinctive groove and feel. In this lesson, we'll explore techniques to improve your sense of timing and rhythm, allowing you to play with confidence and style.

Understanding Blues Rhythm

Blues music is characterized by its unique rhythmic feel, often using a shuffle or swing rhythm that gives the music its laid-back yet driving pulse. Understanding this rhythmic foundation is essential for authentic blues playing.

- **Shuffle Rhythm:** A shuffle rhythm divides each beat into a triplet, with the first two triplet notes combined to create a long-short feel. This gives blues its characteristic swing.
- **Swing Rhythm:** Similar to shuffle, swing emphasizes the off-beat, creating a bouncy and relaxed groove. It's less strict than shuffle, allowing for more personal interpretation.

Timing and Groove

Developing a strong sense of timing is crucial for maintaining the groove in blues music. Here's how to hone your timing skills:

- **Metronome Practice:** Use a metronome to practice playing in time. Start with a slow tempo and gradually increase the speed as you become more comfortable.
- **Tap Your Foot:** Keep time by tapping your foot along with the beat. This physical action helps internalize the rhythm and keeps you grounded in the groove.
- **Counting:** Count out loud or in your head while playing to maintain awareness of the rhythmic structure.

Techniques for Enhancing Rhythm

Incorporating various techniques can enhance your rhythmic playing, adding depth and complexity to your music.

- **Syncopation:** Introduce syncopation by accenting off-beats or unexpected beats, creating rhythmic tension and interest.
- **Ghost Notes:** Use ghost notes, or subtle muted strums, to add texture and groove. These are often played quietly to fill in the rhythmic background.
- **Accents:** Accentuate certain beats or notes to emphasize the rhythm and add dynamic contrast.

To develop your rhythm and timing skills, incorporate these concepts and exercises into your practice routine.By mastering rhythm and timing, you'll become a more versatile and expressive blues guitarist.

These skills are essential for both rhythm playing and soloing, allowing you to create music that grooves and resonates with your audience.

Lesson 28: Riffs into Chord Progressions

Riffs are an essential component of blues music, providing catchy, memorable hooks that can define a song's character. Learning to seamlessly integrate riffs into chord progressions can elevate your rhythm playing and add a distinctive flair to your music.

1. Understanding Riffs in Blues

Riffs are short, repetitive musical phrases that often serve as the backbone of a blues track. They can be simple or complex and are typically used to create a rhythmic and melodic foundation.

- **Role of Riffs:** Riffs provide a catchy motif that listeners can latch onto, often becoming the most recognizable part of a song.
- **Common Usage:** In blues, riffs are frequently used in the introduction, verses, or as a part of the turnaround in a song, adding texture and interest.

2. Crafting Effective Riffs

Creating effective riffs involves balancing simplicity with creativity. Here are some tips for crafting riffs that complement your chord progressions:

- **Start Simple:** Begin with a basic idea, using simple rhythms and note choices. Focus on the groove and feel.
- **Repetition and Variation:** Use repetition to make your riff memorable, but introduce slight variations to maintain interest.
- **Syncopation:** Incorporate syncopation to add rhythmic complexity and drive. This can make your riff more engaging and dynamic.

3. Integrating Riffs into Chord Progressions

To integrate riffs seamlessly into your chord progressions, consider the following approaches:

- **Riff-Based Progressions:** Build your progression around a central riff, allowing it to dictate the rhythm and feel of the song. This approach works well for both rhythm and lead parts.

- **Call and Response:** Use a riff as a "call" that is answered by a chord progression or another riff. This creates a conversational dynamic in your music.
- **Riff Variations:** Modify the riff slightly to fit different parts of the progression, ensuring it complements the changing chords.

Practical Exercises for Riff Integration

To practice integrating riffs into your chord progressions, try these exercises:

- **Riff Composition:** Create a simple riff and practice playing it over a 12-bar blues progression. Focus on timing and how the riff interacts with the chords.
- **Variation Development:** Develop variations of your riff that fit different sections of the progression, such as the turnaround or bridge.
- **Jam Sessions:** Use backing tracks to experiment with inserting riffs into your rhythm playing. Pay attention to how they enhance the overall feel of the music.

*Work with these concepts daily for best results.

Lesson 29: Advanced Rhythm Techniques

As you delve deeper into the world of blues guitar, mastering advanced rhythm techniques will enable you to elevate your playing and bring a new level of sophistication to your music.

Focusing on challenging yourself with advanced rhythmic concepts allows you to add complexity and nuance to your blues performances.

1. Syncopation and Polyrhythms

Syncopation involves placing emphasis on unexpected beats or off-beats, creating rhythmic tension and interest. When effectively used in blues, syncopation can make your music more engaging and dynamic.

- **Off-Beat Accents:** Practice accenting notes on the off-beats to create a syncopated feel. This can be achieved by emphasizing the second and fourth beats in a 4/4 measure.

- **Unexpected Rhythms:** Experiment with syncopated patterns that shift the emphasis away from the downbeat, adding surprise and intrigue to your playing.

Polyrhythms involve playing two or more contrasting rhythms simultaneously. Incorporating polyrhythms into your blues playing can add a layer of complexity and depth.

- **3 Against 2:** Practice playing a triplet rhythm (three notes per beat) against a duplet rhythm (two notes per beat) to develop a polyrhythmic feel.
- **Exploration:** Experiment with different polyrhythmic combinations to discover unique rhythmic textures.

2. Advanced Strumming Patterns

Exploring advanced strumming patterns can enhance your rhythm playing, adding variety and interest to your blues music.

- **Hybrid Picking:** Combine fingerpicking and flatpicking to create intricate and dynamic strumming patterns. This technique allows for greater control and variety in your playing.

- **Percussive Strumming:** Incorporate percussive elements into your strumming by using muted strums or tapping on the guitar body. This adds a rhythmic, drum-like quality to your playing.

3. Dynamic Rhythmic Changes

Dynamic changes in rhythm can transform a piece of music, creating emotional peaks and valleys that captivate listeners.

- **Tempo Shifts:** Practice gradually increasing or decreasing the tempo within a song to build tension or provide relief. This technique requires precise timing and control.
- **Rhythmic Modulation:** Experiment with changing the rhythmic feel of a song, such as transitioning from a shuffle to a straight rhythm, to keep your music fresh and engaging.

By mastering advanced rhythm techniques, you'll expand your musical palette and enhance your ability to create compelling and dynamic blues music.

Lesson 30: Chapter 6 Quiz

Use these questions to review your comprehension of Chapter 6 and ensure you're ready to progress to the next chapter.

Q: What is the basic structure of the 12-bar blues progression?

A: _____

Q: What are two variations of the 12-bar blues?

A: _____

Q: What's the difference between the swing and the shuffle?

A: _____

Q: What is the purpose of practicing with a metronome?

A: _____

Q: What is the benefit of using syncopation in blues rhythms?

A: _____

Q: What are the benefits of using dynamic rhythm changes?

A: _____

Q: How does being proficient at rhythm help your soloing?

A: _____

Chapter 6 Summary

In Chapter 6, you have learned about rhythm progressions in the blues. This is a vital lesson to learn as it allows you to choose the right notes in scales as you harmoniously solo over them.

First, you learned about 3 common blues progressions. The 12-bar blues, the 8-bar blues, and the 16-bar blues. All with something different to offer

Second, you learned about rhythm and timing in the blues. Mastering these elements is crucial for the blues guitarist, as they provide the distinctive groove and feel of the blues.

Third, you learned about riffs into chord progressions. Understanding riffs, creating riffs, and practical exercises for integrating riffs into progressions.

Fourth, you learned about advanced rhythm techniques. Remember, the better understanding of rhythm you acquire, the better a soloist you'll become. Don't forget that.

Fifth, you are presented with a learning assessment to help you analyze your progress and knowledge of the chapter.

Chapter 7 Blues Soloing and Improvisation

Lesson 31: Building a Blues Scale

Building a compelling blues solo is an art form that combines technical skill with emotional expression. A well-crafted solo can capture the listener's attention and convey a powerful narrative through music.

1. Understanding the Structure of a Blues Solo

A successful blues solo often follows a structure that balances tension and release, guiding the listener through a musical journey.

- **Introduction:** Start with a simple idea or motif to set the stage for your solo. This could be a catchy riff or a subtle melodic phrase that introduces the mood.
- **Development:** Gradually build intensity and complexity by expanding on your initial idea. This can involve adding embellishments, changing dynamics, or incorporating faster runs

- **Climax:** Reach a peak in your solo where the emotional intensity is at its highest. This is often achieved through high notes, expressive bends, or rapid sequences.
- **Resolution:** Conclude the solo by returning to a simpler idea or motif, providing a sense of closure and resolving any musical tension.

2. Choosing the Right Scales

Selecting the appropriate scales is crucial for crafting a blues solo that resonates emotionally.

- **Blues Scale:** The quintessential choice for blues solos, with its distinctive blue note adding tension and depth.
- **Minor Pentatonic Scale:** Offers a soulful and melancholic sound, perfect for expressing deeper emotions.
- **Major Pentatonic Scale:** Provides a brighter, more optimistic feel, ideal for solos that convey joy or energy.

Remember, these are the three main scales utilized in playing the blues. Not only can they be used for solos, but they can also be used to create riffs and syncopated rhythms.

The Major Blues Scale

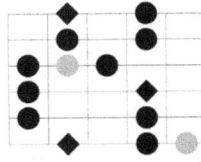 Evokes a bright, bluesy tone.

The Minor Blues Scale

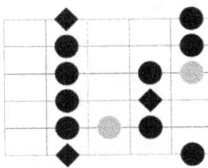 Evokes a somber, bluesy, gritty tone.

The Major Pentatonic Scale

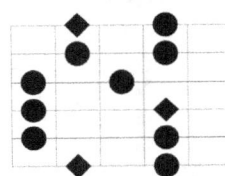 Evokes a bright, pleasant sound.

The Minor Pentatonic Scale

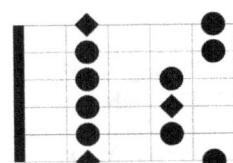 Evokes a dark, sad sound.

Take these emotions into consideration when using these scales to create your musical compositions.

Lesson 32: Techniques for Effective Improvising

Improvisation is a vital component of blues music, allowing you to express your individuality and connect with listeners on a deeper level. Effective improvisation requires a blend of technical skill, creativity, and emotion

This enables you to craft solos that are both spontaneous and captivating. Being able to improvise properly can elevate your blues solos and increase your mastery over the fretboard.

1. Embracing Spontaneity

Improvisation thrives on spontaneity, encouraging you to explore new ideas and follow your instincts.

- **Let Go of Perfection:** Embrace mistakes as opportunities for creativity. Allow your emotions to guide your playing rather than striving for technical perfection.
- **Trust Your Instincts:** Follow your gut feelings during improvisation, letting your musical intuition shape your solos.

2. Building a Foundation with Scales

Having a solid grasp of scales provides the framework for effective improvisation.

- **Blues and Pentatonic Scales:** Use these scales as your primary tools for improvisation, providing familiar ground to explore new ideas.
- **Scale Mastery:** Practice scales in various keys and positions to increase your flexibility and confidence during solos.

3. Experimenting with Rhythms

Rhythmic variation can add intrigue and complexity to your improvisation.

- **Syncopation:** Introduce syncopated rhythms to create unexpected twists and maintain listener interest.
- **Polyrhythms:** Experiment with contrasting rhythms to add depth and complexity to your solos.

The better you know your scales, the better you will be able to use them. They are your lead guitar wizard's tools for creating sounds of mystique and wonder.

4. Developing Melodic Ideas

Crafting strong melodic ideas is essential for engaging improvisations.

- **Motif Variation:** Start with a simple motif and explore variations by altering rhythm, pitch, or dynamics to keep it fresh and engaging.
- **Call and Response:** Use this technique to create a conversational dynamic, adding structure and interaction to your solos.

5. Utilizing Dynamics and Phrasing

Dynamics and phrasing shape the emotional journey of your improvisation.

- **Dynamic Range:** Experiment with different volumes and intensities to convey various emotions and create tension.
- **Phrase Exploration:** Focus on articulating your phrases clearly, using pauses and changes in rhythm for impact.

By mastering these concepts for effective improvisation, you'll be able to craft solos that are rich with emotional creativity. Further enhancing your guitar soloing skills.

Lesson 33: Using Call and Response in Solos

The call and response technique has been mentioned previously, but will be explained in more detail here. It creates a dialogue within the music, engaging both the musician and the listener in a dynamic conversation.

By incorporating call and response into your solos, you can add depth, interaction, and structure to your performance. This lesson will guide you through the process of effectively using call and response in your blues solos.

1. Understanding Call and Response

Call and response is a musical form where a phrase or motif (the "call") is followed by an answering phrase (the "response"). This technique is derived from African musical traditions and has become a defining characteristic of blues music.

- Conversational Dynamic: Call and response creates a back-and-forth interaction, similar to a conversation, which adds a lively and engaging element to your solos.

- **Building Tension and Resolution:** The call often introduces tension or a question, while the response provides resolution or an answer, creating a satisfying musical narrative.

2. Crafting Effective Calls and Responses

To create engaging solos, it's important to craft calls and responses that complement each other and enhance the storytelling aspect of your music.

- **Simple Calls:** Start with a simple, memorable phrase for your call. This could be a short lick or melodic idea that sets the tone for the response.
- **Complementary Responses:** The response should echo or contrast with the call, providing a sense of completion. Experiment with different responses to see what complements the call effectively.

3. Techniques for Call and Response

Incorporating various techniques can enhance your call and response playing, adding complexity and interest to your solos.

- **Dynamic Variation:** Use dynamics to differentiate between the call and response. A soft call followed by a louder response can create a dramatic effect.
- **Rhythmic Contrast:** Vary the rhythm between the call and response to add interest. A syncopated call followed by a straightforward response can create a compelling interplay.
- **Expressive Techniques:** Incorporate bends, slides, and vibrato to add emotional depth to your calls and responses.

By mastering the use of call and response in your blues solos, you'll add a powerful tool to your musical arsenal, enhancing your ability to create expressive and memorable performances.

Lesson 34: Developing a Personal Soloing Style

Creating a personal soloing style is an essential journey for any blues guitarist, allowing you to express your individuality and connect with your audience on a deeper level. Developing your unique voice involves combined techniques.

influences, and personal creativity to craft solos that stand out and resonate emotionally. This lesson will guide you through the process of developing a personal soloing style that reflects your musical identity.

1. Embrace Your Influences

Every guitarist is shaped by the music they love. Embrace these influences and learn from them to help define your unique style.

- **Identify Inspirations:** List your favorite blues guitarists and analyze what aspects of their playing appeal to you. Consider their phrasing, tone, and technique.

- **Learn and Adapt:** Study their solos and incorporate elements that resonate with you into your playing. Adapt these elements to fit your style, ensuring you add your own twist.

2. Experiment with Tone and Gear

Your tone is a crucial element of your soloing style. Explore different gear and settings to find a sound that reflects your personality.

- **Guitar and Amp Settings:** Experiment with your guitar's tone controls and amplifier settings to discover a sound that feels authentic.
- **Effects and Pedals:** Explore effects pedals like overdrive, reverb, or delay to add texture and depth to your sound.

Your guitar and gear can make a huge impact on your artistic creativity. They can help enhance the sounds you are already getting out of the scales. Allowing you to take the blues into uncharted territory.

3. Practice Routine for Style Development

To cultivate your unique soloing style, dedicate time to focused practice sessions.

- **Style Exploration:** Regularly explore different techniques and sounds, allowing your style to evolve naturally.
- **Recording and Reflection:** Record your practice sessions and listen back to assess your style's development. Identify unique elements to refine and expand.
- **Improvisational Practice:** Use backing tracks to practice improvising, allowing your style to emerge as you explore new musical ideas.

To make your solos stand out, focus on expressing emotion through your playing. This connection with the audience is vital. Combine various techniques and embrace your influences to focus on emotional expression.

You'll develop a personal soloing style that reflects your individuality as a guitarist, empowering you to express your musical identity and create a lasting impact in the blues genre.

Lesson 35: Chapter 7 Quiz

Improvising is a great thing to know and master. Especially as a lead guitar player. Test your understanding of Chapter 7 for a full understanding of improvisational concepts.

Q: What are the key stages of a blues solo structure?
A: _____

Q: How can the choice of scales affect the emotion of a solo?
A: _____

Q: Why is embracing spontaneity important in blues soloing?
A: _____

Q: How can syncopation affect the rhythm of a blues solo?
A: _____

Q: Why is the call and response technique important in solos?
A: _____

Q: How can your guitar and gear enhance your blues solos?
A: _____

Q: What is the best way to create your own soloing identity?
A: _____

Chapter 7 Summary

In this chapter, you have learned about blues soloing and improvisation. How to combine technical skill with emotional expression, while capturing the listener's attention.

First, you learned about building a blues solo. Understanding the structure, choosing the right scales, and how they each convey a certain type of emotion.

Second, you learned additional techniques that are used for improvising. Embracing spontaneity, experimenting with scales and rhythms, as well as utilizing phrasing and melodic ideas.

Third, you learned about using call and response in your solos. This creates a musical dialogue. Allowing you to use tension and resolution when crafting with this popular technique.

Fourth, you learned about developing your own personal expression and individuality to create a much deeper connection with your audience.

Fifth, you are presented with a learning assessment. This helps you to define your knowledge, add to your blues foundation, and get you ready for the next chapter.

Chapter 8: More Advanced Concepts

Lesson 36: Improvisational Solo Examples

While learning the scale patterns is just step one, you need to be able to put them into action to get the most from them. That is why in this lesson, examples of soloing phrases will be presented.

By going through these on the guitar, you will have a better understanding of how these magical box patterns can enhance your playing. Not just from a theoretical point of view, but from a practical application point of view.

Guitar Phrasing Examples

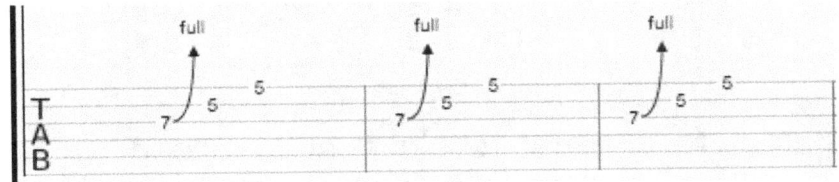

Example 1: Bend the 7th fret on the 3rd string, play the 5th fret on the 2nd and first strings, then repeat.

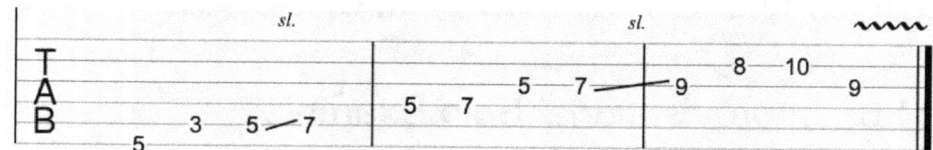

Example 2: Start at the 5th fret, 6th string, and proceed through the scale patterns utilizing slides and vibrato.

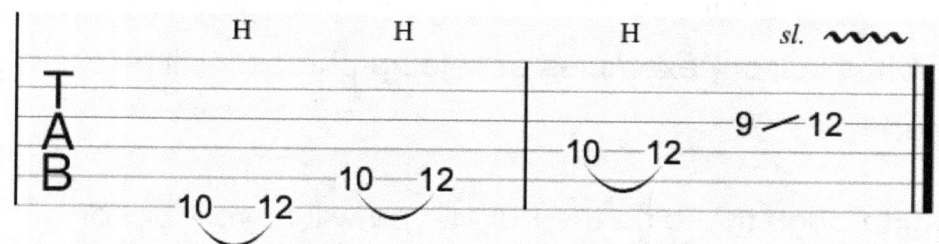

Example 3: Start on the 10th fret 6th string, and proceed through the scale utilizing hammer-ons and vibrato.

Example 4: Start at the 15th fret 1st string, and proceed through the scale utilizing a pull-off and vibrato.

Utilizing Finger Exercises

Finger exercises are a great way to build strength and independence in your fingers.

Example 1: A chromatic run starting at the 5th fret, 1st string to the 8th fret, and using all four fingers on all 6 strings.

Example 2: A chromatic run starting on the open 6th string and proceeding through frets 1,2, and 3, using all four fingers.

Example 3: A chromatic run that spans across four strings.

*Practice these daily to enhance your finger dexterity.

Lesson 37: Using Arpeggios in Blues Solos

Arpeggios are a powerful tool for blues guitarists, offering a way to highlight the harmony of a song while adding depth and complexity to your solos.

By breaking down chords into individual notes, arpeggios provide a framework for exploring the melodic and harmonic possibilities of a progression.

1. Understanding Arpeggios

An arpeggio is a sequence of notes that outlines a chord by playing its notes individually rather than simultaneously. This technique allows guitarists to emphasize the harmonic structure of a song and create more intricate solos.

- **Chord Outlining:** Arpeggios highlight the underlying chord progression, making your solos more connected to the music.
- **Melodic Exploration:** By focusing on individual chord tones, arpeggios offer a framework for developing melodic ideas that complement the harmony.

2. Basic Arpeggio Shapes

Before incorporating arpeggios into your solos, it's essential to familiarize yourself with some basic arpeggio shapes. Here are a few common ones:

- **Major Arpeggio:** Consists of the root, major third, and perfect fifth. For example, a C major arpeggio includes the notes C, E, and G.
- **Minor Arpeggio:** Contains the root, minor third, and perfect fifth. An A minor arpeggio consists of A, C, and E.
- **Dominant 7th Arpeggio:** Includes the root, major third, perfect fifth, and minor seventh. A G7 arpeggio features G, B, D, and F.

C Major Arpeggio: C E G = 1 3 5

A Minor Arpeggio: A C E = 1 flat 3 and 5

Dominant 7th Arpeggio: G B D F = 1 3 5 flat 7

3. Crafting Solos with Arpeggios

Arpeggios can be seamlessly integrated into your solos to add structure and harmonic depth. Here are some techniques to consider:

- **Connecting Chord Tones:** Use arpeggios to connect chord tones within a progression, ensuring your solos feel cohesive and harmonically grounded.
- **Targeting Changes:** Focus on emphasizing the chord changes in a progression by playing the corresponding arpeggio as the chords change.
- **Combining with Scales:** Blend arpeggios with scales, like the blues or pentatonic scales, to create solos that combine melodic fluidity with harmonic clarity.

Incorporating expressive techniques can elevate your arpeggio playing, making your solos more engaging and dynamic. To make arpeggios effective, you must integrate them into your practice routine.

By mastering the use of arpeggios in your blues solos, you'll expand your melodic and harmonic vocabulary.

Lesson 38: Exploring Rock Influence in the Blues

Blues and rock music have shared a symbiotic relationship, with each genre influencing and enriching the other over the decades. By exploring rock influences in blues, you can expand your musical palette and infuse your playing with energy.

1. Understanding the Connection Between Blues and Rock

Rock music has its roots deeply embedded in the blues, borrowing its structures, scales, and emotional depth. Many rock guitarists, such as Jimi Hendrix, Eric Clapton, and Jimmy Page, have drawn inspiration from blues legends, blending these influences to create powerful and enduring music.

- **Shared Scales:** Both genres frequently use the blues scale and minor pentatonic scale, providing a common ground for exploration.
- **Emotional Expression:** Rock amplifies the emotional intensity of blues, often incorporating louder dynamics and more aggressive playing.

2. Rock Techniques to Incorporate into Blues

Integrating rock techniques into your blues playing can add a new dimension to your music. Here are some key techniques to consider:

- **Power Chords:** Use power chords to add a driving, rhythmic foundation to your blues progressions, providing a rock-oriented edge.
- **Distortion and Overdrive:** Experiment with distortion and overdrive effects to create a gritty, powerful sound that enhances the emotional impact of your playing.
- **Aggressive Picking:** Incorporate techniques like palm muting and alternate picking to create a percussive, energetic feel.

Utilizing chords, pedals, and picking hand enhancements will allow you to expand your creativity. By creating enriched landscapes of emotion that could not be done by just ordinary blues guitar playing.

With these types of concepts at your disposal, you can expand the blues into rock n' roll territory and develop a unique style.

3. Crafting Solos with Rock Influences

Rock-influenced solos can bring a fresh, exciting dynamic to your blues playing. Here's how to craft solos that blend these styles:

- **Speed and Precision:** Incorporate faster runs and more precise picking techniques to add excitement and virtuosity to your solos.
- **Wide Bends and Sustained Notes:** Use wide bends and sustain to emphasize key notes, capturing the emotive qualities of both genres.
- **Dynamic Contrasts:** Explore dynamic contrasts by alternating between softer, bluesy phrases and intense, rock-inspired sections.

Rock-influenced solos can bring a fresh, exciting dynamic to your blues playing. Crafting solos and melody lines that blend these styles.

Integrating rock rhythms into your blues playing can also create a distinctive groove that sets your music apart. It's all about the way you choose to approach the instrument.

Lesson 39: The Future of Blues Guitar

The future of blues guitar is an exciting frontier, shaped by innovation and the fusion of diverse musical influences. As blues continues to evolve, it offers endless opportunities.

1. Embracing Technological Advancements

Technology plays a significant role in shaping the future of music, offering new tools and platforms to enhance creativity and reach.

- **Digital Effects and Modeling:** Modern effects pedals and digital modeling devices enable guitarists to explore a vast array of sounds and textures.
- **Music Production Software:** Home recording and production software allow guitarists to create high-quality music independently.
- **Online Collaboration:** The internet facilitates collaboration with musicians worldwide, encouraging the exchange of ideas and the blending of different styles to create innovative blues music.

2. Exploring Unconventional Techniques

Pushing the boundaries of technique is essential for the continued evolution of blues guitar.

- **Extended Techniques:** Incorporate tapping, harmonics, and fingerstyle techniques to create complex and engaging solos.
- **Innovative Picking Styles:** Experiment with hybrid picking or alternate tunings to discover new sounds and possibilities within the blues framework.

3. Fusion with Other Genres

Blues has always been an adaptable genre, and its future will likely involve further fusion with other musical styles.

- **Jazz and Blues Fusion:** Combining the improvisational elements of jazz with blues can lead to sophisticated and harmonically rich compositions.
- **Blues and Hip-Hop:** Integrating the rhythmic and lyrical aspects of hip-hop with traditional blues can create fresh and culturally relevant music.

3. Cultivating a Personal Voice

In a genre as expressive as blues, cultivating a personal voice is crucial for making a lasting impact.

- **Authenticity and Emotion:** Focus on conveying genuine emotion through your playing, as this connection with the audience is the heart of blues music.
- **Innovation and Tradition:** Balance innovation with respect for the genre's roots, ensuring that your contributions honor the blues tradition while pushing it forward.

4. Engaging with the Blues Community

The blues community plays a vital role in preserving and promoting the genre.

- **Live Performances:** Participate in live performances, jam sessions, and festivals to connect with other musicians and audiences, sharing your unique sound and vision.
- **Education and Mentorship:** Contribute to the education and mentorship of emerging blues musicians, helping to nurture the next generation of blues talent.

Lesson 40: Chapter 8 Quiz

Once again, we have a simple assessment exercise (or quiz) to make sure you know the material in this chapter.

Q: What is the benefit of improvisational solo examples?

A: _____

Q: What types of techniques are common in solo examples?

A: _____

Q: How can arpeggios enhance your blues guitar soloing?

A: _____

Q: What are the benefits of combining arpeggios and scales?

A: _____

Q: How can power chords and pedals enhance your soloing?

A: _____

Q: What is the role of rock rhythms in blues music?

A: _____

Q: Why is the future of blues music important to you?

A: _____

Chapter 8 Summary

In this final chapter, you have learned about advanced concepts that will allow you to take the scales that you have learned in the training and put them into practical application.

First, you are presented with phrasing examples. These utilize the techniques you learned earlier. Allowing you to see how they are used in a musical landscape.

Second, you learned about using arpeggios in solos. These are a great way to mix rhythm and melody together. As well as increase your knowledge of timing and rhythm.

Third, at chord switching. This is essential for playing rhythm guitar. The better you can do this, the more fluid your playing will be.

Fourth, you explored the connection between rock and the blues. How they are closely related and what scales work best with each style of music.

Fifth, you are presented with the last and final assessment of the course. If you've mastered these, you have risen above 99% of the guitar players out there.

Demystifying the Blues Scales Conclusion

Congratulations on completing "Demystifying The Blues Scales," a comprehensive journey through the rich and emotive world of blues guitar. As you've explored each chapter, you've unlocked the secrets of this timeless genre.

This guide has equipped you with the essential concepts and techniques that form the foundation of blues music. Exploring the blues scales, the minor and major pentatonics, you will be provided with the melodic tools to craft authentic blues sounds.

Thank you for embarking on this journey through the blues. May your guitar playing be forever enriched by the knowledge and inspiration you've gained along the way. Keep exploring, and you'll keep the blues alive.

If you have any questions about anything you've learned in this course, contact me through my website. I will be happy ot help.

DwaynesGuitarLessons.com

Best of luck and have fun.
Sincerely, Dwayne Jenkins

All books are authored by Dwayne Jenkins and can be found on Amazon or wherever books are sold worldwide.

These can also be found on Dwayne's website in digital format for quicker learning. Just download it onto your computer and start learning right away.

Online courses are also available with comprehensive video instruction that can easily be learned by anyone. With lifelong access, you can study at any time from anywhere.

Self-study is a great way to learn, as it allows you to not only go at your own pace but also develop the skills of discipline and time management. These can help benefit you in other areas of your life as well.

If more help is needed, Dwayne also offers one-on-one private coaching. Which can also be found on his website.

Also, be sure to check out Dwayne's video lessons on YouTube. These are free and available 24 hours a day, 7 days a week, 365 days a year.

Thanks again, Tritone Publishing © 2025.
All Rights Reserved.

About the Author

Dwayne Jenkins is a professional guitar teacher and an accomplished musician. He has been learning, playing, and teaching guitar lessons throughout Denver, CO, for over two decades.

Dwayne has a unique, exciting approach that gets students of all ages and skill levels enjoying the fun of playing guitar. His enthusiasm and love for teaching shine through with every lesson that he creates.

His lessons are designed to enhance your ability to progress. No matter your reason for learning, there will always be something in Dwayne's books and online courses to help you reach your goal of becoming a proficient guitarist.

Students benefit from Dwayne's extensive experience and passion for music, which fosters a supportive and inspiring learning environment. Encouraging creative expression and helping students build confidence in their musical abilities.

Providing an invaluable opportunity to develop a lifelong appreciation for learning and playing the guitar with joy.

What Students Are Saying About Dwayne's Guitar Lessons

"Dwayne, thank you so much for everything you have taught me and done for me. You are an amazing guitarist and wonderful teacher," BJ.

"Dwayne, it has been a true pleasure to have you at our house each week! Ken & Trevor have learned so much through you and your teachings. Thank you!" Lisa.

"Dwayne, thank you for being a great teacher and teaching me many great songs. This is a skill that will last me a lifetime." Danielle.

"Dwayne, we want you to know we are honored to have you at the studio. We appreciate all that you do and are grateful that we can leave you in charge," Angie & Wilson M.E.C.

"Dwayne, we are so glad you are our Teacher. It's been three years already, can you believe it? Thank you again. You're the best!" Chelsey & Lucas.

"Dwayne, we are so glad that you are in our lives. Chelsey & Lucas enjoy their time with you and look up to you. Looking forward to another great year!" Love and best wishes, Ken & Sue.

"Dwayne, thank you so much for being not only an awesome guitar teacher, but an awesome friend as well," Kayla.

"Dwayne, thank you so much for all the years of doing lessons. You have been very patient with my progress, helped me to build confidence in myself, and inspired me to follow my dreams. And in doing so, you have become a great friend," Jake.

"Dwayne, thank you for teaching Nick guitar so well. He loves it and is getting quite good fast. I'm amazed!" Jane.

"Dwayne, thank you so much for teaching me every Saturday and not only teaching me guitar but also about life, and helping me with setting my goals. You are a great teacher, mentor, and the best friend ever," Carson.

"There is no other person I would want to teach me guitar! His 1-on-1 teaching makes learning guitar very personal & exhilarating. He teaches at your pace and takes pride in what YOU want to learn.

The best part...if Dwayne doesn't know a song a student wants to play, he takes time out of the week to learn it. His teaching comes to life in my performance and has progressed over the last 8 years. Words cannot describe how amazing a teacher, rockstar, and true friend Dwayne has become to me," Dominic.